THE MURDERER,
THE MONARCH
AND THE FAKIR

THE MURDERER, THE MONARCH AND THE FAKIR

A New Investigation of
Mahatma Gandhi's
Assassination

APPU ESTHOSE SURESH
AND
PRIYANKA KOTAMRAJU

HarperCollins *Publishers* India

First published in India by
HarperCollins *Publishers* 2021
A-75, Sector 57, Noida, Uttar Pradesh 201301, India
www.harpercollins.co.in

2 4 6 8 10 9 7 5 3 1

P-ISBN: 978-93-5489-053-6
E-ISBN: 978-93-5489-061-1

Typeset in 11.5/15.7 Warnock Pro at
Manipal Technologies Limited, Manipal

Printed and bound at
Thomson Press (India) Ltd

To all the unnamed sources.
And to all our teachers.

Contents

Book III
The Fakir

Prologue

'ON 30 January 1948, Mahatma Gandhi was assassinated by a fanatic, Nathuram Godse, because he disagreed with Gandhiji's conviction that Hindus and Muslims should live together in harmony[1].'

Arguably modern India's biggest political development, the assassination of Mahatma Gandhi finds a desultory mention in our school history textbooks. These lines from the National Council of Educational Research and Training (NCERT) textbook were the closest I got to understanding a pivotal moment in India's history. History, for me at least, was taught as a collection of bald facts. We learned dates, events and names of people, and hardly anything else. Despite its rather anodyne presentation in our texts, history fascinated me; in fact, it still does.

I joined St. Stephen's college in New Delhi for my graduation. I was a resident of the Rudra North Block residence hall, which was named after the first Indian principal of the college—and perhaps the first Indian principal of a missionary college anywhere—Sushil Kumar Rudra. Suddenly, history became part and parcel of everyday life. As a fresher (or fuchcha in university parlance), the initiation process involved me getting to know everything about the college, my dorm, its previous occupants, even the number of trees on the campus. Possession of these historical facts guaranteed my safe passage into the college brotherhood. What I didn't realize then was that these silly rites of passage had brought me closer to knowing Mohandas Karamchand Gandhi than ever before.

That C.F. Andrews, also known as Deenabandhu, was instrumental in bringing Gandhi from South Africa to India was just another interesting but incomplete factoid from our textbooks. It was only after joining the college that I began to realize the enormous significance of this. In 1913, S.K. Rudra sent his vice-principal C.F. Andrews to South Africa to persuade Gandhi to return to India. Andrews spent six months there, eventually succeeding in his mission. When Gandhi arrived in Delhi, it was Rudra's home that offered him shelter, despite the misgivings of and warnings by the imperial government. It was under Principal Rudra's roof that Gandhi shaped the Khilafat movement and the non-cooperation movement.

In 1925, Gandhi wrote, 'The reader may not be aware that my open letter to the Viceroy, giving concrete shape to the Khilafat claim, was conceived and drafted under Principal Rudra's roof. He and Charlie Andrews were my revisionists. Non-cooperation was conceived and hatched under his hospitable roof.'[2] It was also thanks to Andrews that Gandhi met Rabindranath Tagore and became great friends. Piecing together these nuggets one by one brought me closer to understanding the overarching arc of history of Delhi and India at the time.

Despite its pivotal role in shaping modern Indian history and its deep association with Gandhi, St. Stephen's had let dust settle on these chapters. The Gandhi Study Circle (GSC), which was one of the oldest student societies, was practically defunct when I joined. In hindsight, the GSC's inactivity was in some ways a reflection of what has happened to Gandhi and Gandhian thought in modern India. I was fortunate enough to be one of the small group of students who revived this society in our college. We got K.P. Shankaran, then head of the philosophy department, as its staff advisor. This was a big deal, because K.P. Shankaran is an authority on Gandhian thought and political philosophy. Over the years, we have had many exchanges on Gandhi. One particular conversation comes to mind, which forms the foundational inquiry of this book. 'You have to ask yourself which Gandhi you are investigating ... If you read Godse's reasons for assassinating Gandhi, he's talking about an entirely different entity. Godse killed a man who he thought was a traitor to his faith and his people—someone who did not support the Indian state and was an anti-national.'[3]

Shankaran said that the Gandhi who is the Father of the Nation is a construction of the Government of India and modern Indian historians of all persuasions—left, right, and centre. According to him, Gandhi was against the formation of the Indian state. He was not a religious person, but he used

Hindu vocabulary to get ordinary Hindus to practise what he called an ethical religion. Shankaran also posited that the issue of Hindu masculinity should be understood in the context of 'Gandhi's rejection of the Indian population as cowards and therefore unethical. Gandhi has a very significant theory which links fear and an unethical life. Unethical life here means preoccupation with oneself.' He asked me to carefully listen to V. Madhusoodanan Nair's poem on Gandhi.[4]

We are not historians, or philosophers, or poets. But Nair's poem, even to the untrained ear, is a powerful portrayal of the many Gandhis we might claim to know. One Gandhi is the man who walks alone on a path so difficult that even his followers, the anugami, fail to accompany him. There is another Gandhi, the one who fell into a 'burning clay pot' of his own making—perhaps this refers to the Gandhi who strove for religious pluralism all his life to fall to the bullet of a religious fanatic. Then there is the Gandhi who springs up occasionally from the pages of our history books as the Father of the Nation or the architect of a national movement. There is the Gandhi who marched to Dandi as an act of civil disobedience to teach us to be our own masters and unshackle ourselves from slavery. There is also the Gandhi who was a flicker of light that remained undimmed in all weathers; indefatigable and steadfast in a purpose that he alone best understood. At one point, the poet asks if Gandhi is a dream or a story we might have heard, because of how implausible his goals were. Who is/was Gandhi? The one who sparked love and admiration in millions? The one who willingly sacrificed his frail body for satyagraha? The one who was able to tame the wildest among the Indians of his time and bring them together? Or is Gandhi the one who absorbed the trauma and shattered hopes of hundreds and thousands of people? There is that Gandhi for whom God is not Rama or Christ or Allah; God is love. In the final denouement, Nair writes that there may be multiple ways of knowing and seeing him, but Gandhi transcends even those expectations and perceptions. It does not matter how we write or rewrite him; he is what he is.

I repeated parts of this conversation to one of my sources, who was an erudite third-generation bureaucrat with a keen memory for details. He told me that several years ago he had seen a picture of the Maharaja of Alwar, whose nails had grown rather long, in house arrest imposed by then Home Minister Sardar Vallabhbhai Patel. The senior bureaucrat believed that the gun that killed Gandhi came from the Alwar armoury. This turned out to be one of the many conspiracies about the assassination, best classified as unverifiable rumours. There, in March 2013, began my search for the gun that killed Gandhi. This anecdote rekindled my interest in Gandhi, especially in the reasons for his murder, and the involvement of all the actors in the conspiracy. As a journalist, I had some idea that the political climate was also about to change, which only increased my curiosity.

I went about this story just as I would pursue any other investigation. The first hurdle for me was the discovery that no one repository housed the Gandhi assassination files; they were scattered haphazardly between the National Archives of India and the Nehru Memorial Museum Library (NMML). As an investigative journalist, my routine was to go beyond what was publicly available, be it documents, file notations or conversations. I wanted to know facts about the assassination that were not publicly accessible. The National Archives and NMML were great starting points. A third great source was the Jeevan Lal Kapur Commission report. This commission of inquiry came about because of a statement issued by G.V. Ketkar, the editor of *Tarun Bharat*, former editor of *Kesari* and grandson of freedom fighter Bal Gangadhar Tilak, in 1964. He was speaking on the occasion of a meeting organized to felicitate Gopal Godse and Vishnu Karkare on the completion of their jail term for their role in Gandhi's assassination. According to an *Indian Express* report of 14 November 1964, Ketkar claimed that he had known about the assassination plot many weeks in advance, a statement he later revised from knowing about the 'actual plot' to knowing about the 'intention'. The Kapur Commission report contained many details and its exhibits were a great source. However, the commission focused more on the lapses in the probe. Sure, it did bring out the fact that V.D. Savarkar, the Hindutva icon who was acquitted for lack of evidence, was in touch with those who were directly involved in the assassination plot before it was carried out. Savarkar's bodyguard Appa Ramachandra Kasar and secretary Gajanan Vishnu Damle did reveal this to the Bombay police, but it was never brought to trial.[5] Had this evidence been presented during the trial, the outcome of it might have been different.

Another good source was Manohar Malgonkar's *The Men Who Killed Gandhi*, where the author had access to some of the accused and the material from the Kapur Commission report. Briefly, in our understanding, many of the books that have discussed the assassination so far have been based on either the evidence or arguments during trials, or the Kapur Commission Report or interviews of the accused themselves. But in our opinion, those who could have told the real story were only the two who were given capital punishment—Nathuram Godse and Narayan Apte. For us, there was only one option left: to find out who else came close to unveiling this heinous plot. The answer was a pretty straightforward one—the investigators of the case.

The first step was to identify the potential sources—the intelligence bureau (IB), the state intelligence departments and the crime investigation department (CID). An insight into the functioning of these agencies helped immensely. Many intelligence briefs were already declassified. A deep research into those files helped secure the first batch of connected intelligence notes for the purpose of this book. It was during this research that we realized what a treasure trove of historical evidence was lying waste in some police record rooms. Being an active journalist covering the government in Delhi helped gain access to some of the places, which are otherwise not easily accessible to researchers.

But that was also one of my biggest challenges: to be in a high-pressure outcome-oriented job and manage the research side by side. It came down to planning. Every government file, even the top-secret notes, had an initiator. In the period between 1948–50, just after Independence, police and intelligence departments were loosely interconnected. It was easier to obtain information on government files and notes from police stations and offices that were far flung, not situated in Delhi. I therefore started focusing on stories that would enable me to spend more time in the record rooms and thus help me know more about the keeping of files within these intelligence establishments. During these years, I followed one story year after year from 2014–2016—the riot series. I started documenting small-scale riots spurting in different parts of India and reporting on them from ground zero. These reports provided excellent opportunities for me to build sources and collect information from the state intelligence departments and the CID. I chose those districts that figured in the first batch of intelligence notes, which gave leads of the conspiracy. Most of them were dead ends. But some of them were not. It was much easier to access the record rooms in these smaller district headquarters than accessing them from the nerve centre in Delhi.

In 2014, a controversy broke out that the Gandhi Assassination Files had been weeded out.[6] The then Home Minister Rajnath Singh denied any such incident. However, it hastened my efforts to gather as much information as possible at the earliest. Tracing some of the family members of those who were part of the investigation team and making contact was the most difficult assignment in my reporting career.

Similarly, during my time in London during 2017–18 as a Residential Fellow at LSE, I went through the list of foreign correspondents, those who had covered Gandhi's assassination, to look for some leads. I was hoping for some confidential files tucked away in a trunk. The declassified files in the National Archives of London were also of great assistance. By 2018, thanks to all these sources, I had enough material and perspective to start stitching the larger picture. By that time, Priyanka Kotamraju had also joined me in the search.

For us however, there remained two unanswered questions: Why investigate Gandhi's assassination today? What is new that we are bringing out seventy years after the assassination?

*

For Priyanka and me, it made sense to revisit Gandhi's assassination. The current national political churn that we are witnessing feels familiar. This was the tension that animated the politics at the time of Independence and, we believe, it was the motivation for Mahatma Gandhi's murder. What would be the character of our nationalism post-Independence? We have tried to understand this dilemma using a framework of 'lack', or what Slavoj Žižek calls the 'theft of enjoyment'. In our understanding, 'lack' explains both ideas of nationalism—the one envisioned by Gandhi and the one by Savarkar. Gandhian nationalism, as Shankaran explained, was driven by the need to be ethical and moral by upholding ahimsa and truth, whereas violence was a sign of weakness and cowardice. Savarkar's nationalism was driven by another kind of 'lack', an anxious masculinity, in which Hindus possessed no self-awareness, were disunited, and had not militarized—qualities he imputed on to communities that became the 'other'.

To quote Žižek,

> The national Cause is ultimately nothing but the way subjects of a given ethnic community organize their enjoyment through national myths. What is therefore

at stake in ethnic tensions is always the possession of the national Thing. We always impute to the 'other' an excessive enjoyment; s/he wants to steal our enjoyment (by ruining our way of life) and/or has access to some secret, perverse enjoyment. In short, what really bothers us about the 'other' is the peculiar way it organizes its enjoyment: precisely the surplus, the 'excess' that pertains to it—the smell of their food, their 'noisy' songs and dances, their strange manners, their attitude to work (in the racist perspective, the 'other' is either a workaholic stealing our jobs or an idler living on our labour). The basic paradox is that our Thing is conceived as something inaccessible to the other, and at the same time threatened by it ...

Using this framework, Priyanka and I have tried to understand how Savarkar conceptualized Hindutva, why the idea of the 'other' is so central to the definition of who is a Hindu, and why the narrative of '*Hindu khatre mein hai*' resonates from the Somnath Temple in the eleventh century to Moplah in the 1920s, the Partition in 1947 until even today. We have then tried to understand which Gandhi was assassinated—the anti-national or the apostle of non-violence or the one for whom God was love, not Rama, not Allah.

Appu Esthose Suresh
August 2021, New Delhi

Book I
The Murderer

1

The August Conspiracy

8 August 1947

AIR India's propeller aircraft DN-438 took off from Bombay (now Mumbai). Delhi, the new national capital, was the destination.[1] For centuries, Delhi had been the seat of power. In 1947, Delhi's power (the British empire) stretched from the treacherous mountains of the North West Frontier Province bordering Afghanistan in the west to the deep jungles bordering Burma (now Myanmar) in the east. This was about to change. The sun had set on the British Empire in south Asia; two new independent nations were about to be born and torn asunder at the same time in the bloodiest of violence.

The British crown and its government did not think much of India and its new political leadership. They were very sure that the country's experiment with democracy would result in failure and it would disintegrate into hundreds of little kingdoms and principalities. Governing India was an experience of a lifetime—it was unmanageably large and rooted in complex and rigid social hierarchies that made decision-making a nightmare. Even for a foreign colonial empire, with absolute power over this vast land, governing had never been easy. And now the young political leadership of India, with little experience in governance, was going to make a grand experiment with parliamentary democracy.

In any transformation, there are winners and losers. In August 1947, while India and Pakistan had won independence, millions of Hindus, Muslims, Sikhs and other communities—inhabitants of this land—had lost lives, families, properties and honour. But that's another story.

Onboard DN-438 were three passengers, representing the interests of those who had lost out in the new, independent India—the privileged Hindus, mostly represented by the Hindu Mahasabha. The Hindu Mahasabha, a socio-political organization, had taken the middle path during the freedom struggle and thus failed to secure a seat at the high table. Princes and maharajas of princely states, who had ruled India in the past and maintained their elite positions in the British Raj, also lost out. However, the Mahasabha and the rulers of the princely states believed that they were custodians of Hindu culture and consequently, the rightful inheritors of power in India, which became a Hindu-majority nation after the Partition.

4

There was no invitation forthcoming to the Mahasabha and princely states to share power in the new India, but that was not sufficient reason to stop them from attempting to secure it.

On 9 August, British lawyer and civil servant Sir Cyril John Radcliffe, who was tasked with the division of India, drew a border on lands he had not fully seen. There was an uneasy air in Delhi. Along with freedom, everyone anticipated chaos. The ensuing confusion offered a lot of possibilities, but there was one man standing in the way of our three travellers—a fakir, Mahatma Gandhi.

Who were these three passengers aboard DN-438? Vinayak Damodar Savarkar, the father of Hindutva and founder of Hindu Mahasabha, accompanied by two of his trusted lieutenants, Nathuram Godse and Narayan Apte, members of the Mahasabha and publishers of the *Hindu Rashtra* newspaper. The official reason for the journey was to attend the All India Hindu Mahasabha Working Committee meeting, the organization over which Savarkar had presided from 1937 to 1945. But for the past several months, his health had been declining. He had stopped accepting any invitation that required him to travel outside of Bombay. Yet, he had chosen to travel to Delhi. This must have been an important trip.

*

Vinayak Damodar Savarkar, affectionately called Tatya, was born on 28 May 1883 in Bhagur, a small town close to Nashik in Maharashtra, to a family of nationalistic Chitpavan Brahmins. He was a politically conscious person from very early on; along with Trinbak Rao Mahaskar and Raoji Krisna Paage he started the Mitra Mela, which was renamed as Abhinav Bharat Society in 1904. His brother Ganesh or Babarao was an active member too. Members of this society were behind the murder of Sir Curzon Wyllie. Ganesh was sentenced to life imprisonment in the Andamans for his activities, as was Savarkar later.[2] While in the UK, studying law, Savarkar was part of the India House, which became a hub for political activism. One of the first books he wrote was on the 1857 revolt, which he called the first revolutionary war for independence. The book was banned by the British. Savarkar was arrested in 1910 for his connections with India House and upon his arrival in India was sentenced to two life terms at the notorious Cellular Jail in the Andamans. A few months into his incarceration, where he was classed as a 'D' (dangerous) prisoner, Savarkar made an about-turn and pleaded for clemency from the British government, promising his loyalty: 'I for one cannot but be the staunchest advocate of constitutional progress and loyalty to the English government.'[3] In 1921, he was released to a prison in Ratnagiri. Over the next few years, Savarkar wrote his seminal work, *Essentials of Hindutva*, in which he introduces and defines Hindutva, the political ideology that has come to shape our national discourse. It was during this time that he met a young Nathuram Godse, who became his follower. In the late 1920s, Savarkar became actively involved with the Hindu Mahasabha, charting an irreversible political course for the organization. The Hindu Mahasabha was an outfit dedicated to the Hindu community, with a following of a million Hindus. By the early twentieth century, Hindu nationalism had emerged as a feature of politics in northern India. Its ideology was represented by the Mahasabha, which originated in Punjab and culminated in the establishment of the All India Hindu Mahasabha in 1915. The Mahasabha's politics diverged from the Congress; its discourse focused mainly on anti-Muslim hostility, which saw the presence of Muslims as the primary obstacle to the creation of a Hindu nation.

In 1948, after Mahatma Gandhi's assassination, Savarkar was named as a co-conspirator but was never charged due to lack of sufficient evidence. After decades of being lost in the political wilderness, he has re-emerged in contemporary India, and his formulation of political Hindutva has found many takers. Despite Savarkar being a staunch opponent to Gandhi and his moral and political philosophy, and having a direct link to his assassination, the image of Savarkar is undergoing a rapid rehabilitation in today's times.

Back in August 1947, Savarkar had come out of retirement to make the journey to Delhi. He had grown old and his prolonged illness had left him fragile. He had hidden himself away in Bombay. But even then, he was a prominent figure and a prolific writer. He inspired a generation of Hindu leaders towards the militant mobilization of the Hindus.

*

Nathuram Godse was born on 19 May 1910 into a poor orthodox Brahmin family, near Poona (now Pune), Maharashtra. The family believed that their male children were under a curse— three sons had died one after the other. In order to ward off this 'curse', Nathuram was raised as a girl in his formative years and his nose was pierced, hence the name Nathuram—

the boy who survived the curse.[4] He was a voracious reader, but unfortunately he could not pass his matriculation exam. When his father, a postmaster, was transferred to Ratnagiri in 1929, nineteen-year-old Godse rejoiced. He had read that Vinayak Damodar Savarkar, who was sentenced to life imprisonment by the British in Andamans, had been shifted to the small, sleepy town. Author Manohar Malgonkar notes that within three days of his arrival in Ratnagiri, Godse went to meet Savarkar.[5]

That meeting changed Godse's life. He became devoted to Savarkar and blindly followed the Hindutva leader's ideology that spanned social, political and religious fields. It has been reported that Nathuram requested to read Savarkar's Hindu Mahasabha speeches to prepare his final statement before execution.

Savarkar was forty-six years old and Godse was nineteen when they met. Even though he was asked to refrain from political writing, it was in this period that Savarkar wrote not just *Essentials of Hindutva*, but also a loose fictionalized account of the Moplah riots in 1921–22 (described in detail in Book 3, 'The Fakir'). The ideas in both these books have immeasurably shaped the Hindutva project and the ideology of Hindu masculinity.

In 1937, Bombay Presidency got its first elected government. One of the first acts of this government was to release Savarkar. Savarkar's return from Ratnagiri to Bombay turned into a victory tour, filled with lectures and public appearances en route. Godse accompanied Savarkar on this tour. Gradually, he was drawn into Hindu Sangathan activities and then

Mahasabha activities. It was also at this time that Vinayak Damodar Savarkar became 'Veer' Savarkar, an appellation bestowed upon him by his followers. In 1938, Godse was given the charge to lead the Mahasabha in a protest march against Hyderabad state for its treatment of Hindu citizens. He was arrested and sent to a year's imprisonment.

As a member of the Mahasabha, Godse rose through the ranks very quickly, thanks to his mentor Savarkar. In 1938–39, he was joint secretary of the Poona city branch of the Mahasabha; a year later he was made secretary. Two years later, he made it to the Maharashtra Provincial Hindu Sabha as its secretary. In 1944–45, he became a member of the All India Hindu Mahasabha. He became a member on the Executive Committee of the Maharashtra Provincial Hindu Sabha in 1947–48.

The trip from Bombay to Delhi on 8 August 1947, was not the first time Godse had accompanied Savarkar. Between 1938 and 1943, he used to go with Savarkar whenever the latter was on tour.[6]

During the period when Savarkar was at the helm of the Hindu Mahasabha, Hindutva politics took shape and also saw many churnings. For the first time, the Rashtriya Swayamsevak Sangh (RSS) came out of his shadow and laid the foundation for long-term survival. It was Savarkar who had inspired Keshav Baliram Hedgewar to found the RSS in 1925. The Hindu Mahasabha was inherently elite in its nature; it was organized around and by prominent Hindus. It failed to become a mass organization like the Indian National Congress. One of the objectives of the formation of the RSS was for it to have a mass base.

In 1941, Godse met Narayan Dattatraya Apte when the latter visited the Mahasabha party office in Poona. A year younger to Godse, the two could not have been more different. Godse was an austere man, sworn to celibacy and the Hindu cause. He led a very simple life, with few wants and needs. On the other hand, Narayan Apte was flamboyant. He came from a better-off middle-class Brahmin family, and was educated and worldly. He had a graduate degree, drank, smoked and had a bit of a roving eye. Apte enjoyed watching films. He even had a king's commission in the Royal Indian Air Force.[7] He was married with two daughters.

Godse and Apte, as different as chalk and cheese, became the closest of friends. In 1942, when Godse set up the Hindu Rashtra Dal, a fringe right-wing outfit, Apte joined him. Two years later, in 1944, when Godse started a newspaper by the name of *Dainik Agrani* (later renamed to *Hindu Rashtra*), Apte joined him there as well. Godse was the editor and Apte the manager.

Apte and Godse shared an almost familial bond; only a week before the assassination of Mahatma Gandhi, in January 1948, Godse had transferred his life insurance policy to Apte's wife and his younger brother, Gopal.

Nathuram Godse was a close disciple of Savarkar. Apte became Godse's close friend and aide, but did not rise to an official position in the Hindu Mahasabha. It seems understandable that Godse accompanied Savarkar on this trip. But why was Apte with them? It was not possible that he had been invited to the working committee meeting of the All India Hindu Mahasabha. He had a lot of work in sales and fundraising for the *Hindu Rashtra* though. This was serious work; there was already a hefty penalty on the newspaper for violating the Indian Press (Emergency) Act because of inflammatory articles that contributed to communal hatred.

If one were to look for a common thread that bound these three passengers, then one would find it in their deep, unwavering resentment of Gandhi and his politics.

In July 1944, Gandhi went to Panchgani, a hill resort barely 50 kilometres from Poona, for his annual retreat. It was here that Narayan Apte led a team of his followers to stage a demonstration and confront Gandhi about the partition of India that was to come. On 23 July 1944, the *Times of India* reported the news with the headline, 'Mr Gandhi Heckled', and mentioned that Poona journalist N.D. Apte was the leader of this demonstration. The *Dainik Agrani* also reported the incident, albeit in a different light. It carried an article on the front page, with a photograph of Apte bearing the caption, 'I Denounce You a Hundred Times Because You Have Conceded Pakistan!'[8] Apte was detained by the police, and his opposition to Gandhi and his politics was on record since 1944.

Before embarking on the August 1947 trip, Apte went to meet Digambar Badge in Ahmednagar, one of the conspirators who turned approver in the Gandhi assassination case. Badge was the owner and proprietor of Shastra Bhandar in Poona. He was a known arms dealer and became a member of the Hindu Rashtra Dal at the end of 1946 or the beginning of 1947. Badge started Shastra Bhandar in 1942; since then he had been selling arms, ammunition and explosives to support the Hindu cause from Kashmir to Hyderabad. He was prosecuted three times under the Arms Act but also acquitted every time. According to Badge, Apte met him towards the end of July 1947 and 'requested him for arranging to get him some arms and he secured one sten-gun for him for Rs 1200 [sic]'.[9]

Apte, according to one version, wanted a Sten gun to wipe out the entire Pakistani leadership in a one-man act while the Pakistani Constituent Assembly was in session in Delhi. However, as Badge confessed later, there was another version. Apte told him he had approached the arms dealer on behalf of 'influential persons'. At the time of procuring the Sten gun, Apte was accompanied by Vishnu Karkare, yet another member of this oddly assembled squad. Karkare had been the Hindu Mahasabha secretary in Ahmednagar since 1938; he was more of a behind-the-scenes organizer. At first, Apte and Karkare were a bit wary of Badge. It took them time to be able to work together smoothly.

Upon arrival in Delhi, Godse and Apte met with another militant Hindu leader called Dattatreya Parchure from Gwalior, another key link to the murder of Mahatma Gandhi. Parchure, a doctor by practice, was a Hindutva strongman in Gwalior. He ran his own outfit called the Hindu Rashtra Sena (HRS). The Hindu Mahasabha's internal document sheds more light on the nature of its association with Parchure. A ledger documenting the activities of the Hindu Mahasabha, updated on 13 March 1945, lists Parchure as a prominent worker. Under the sub-head 'militarization' the document mentions, 'Hindu Rashtra Sena having 200 boys + 12 Akharas having 200 men. They are not under the control of the Sabha but the H.R.S (Hindu Rashtra Sena) works for Hindutva.' [sic] For his part, Savarkar had a perfect cover for his visit to Delhi, which he put forth later in his defence:

I wished that two leading organizations, the Congress and the Mahasabha, which were in fact coming very close to each other, should form a common front and strengthen the hands of the Central Government of our State. To that end I accepted the new National Flag. Though ill, I went to preside over the All Party Hindu Conference at Delhi and attended the Mahasabha Working Committee. The Mahasabha Working Committee passed a resolution to back up the Central Government.[10]

However, the August 1947 meeting of the Working Committee of the All India Hindu Mahasabha was extremely significant for another reason. This was the first time that all the accused and co-conspirators of Gandhi's assassination met. Each of them was intertwined directly with the network that was part of Gandhi's murder, covertly and overtly; directly and indirectly.

Dattatreya Parchure arranged for the Beretta gun that was used by Nathuram Godse to kill Gandhi. Narayan Apte was in charge of the logistics. Vishnu Karkare recruited Madanlal Pahwa, the refugee who was arrested after the failed assassination attempt on 20 January. Vinayak Damodar Savarkar was their guiding spirit. A Criminal Investigation

Department (CID) intelligence note from the morning of 30 January 1948 best establishes the interconnections between the killers of Gandhi.[11]

Rambharose Singh, a head constable with the CID Lashkar, in Gwalior, filed a report to the sub-inspector in charge. Singh had been with the CID for fifteen years. Since 1946, he was tasked with collecting intelligence related to the Hindu Mahasabha, which also included Mahasabha activities and those of affiliate organizations such as the Hindu Rashtra Sena and the RSS. Singh attended organization meetings and submitted reports regarding the arrival and departure of outstation and local Hindu Mahasabha leaders to his superiors. In these two years, Singh had developed a network of sources among Mahasabha workers. On 29 January 1948, a source tipped him off about two visitors who had come from Bombay to Dattatreya Parchure's house on the previous day.

> My source was a close associate of Dr. Parchure and as such, he told me that he wanted to see Dr. Parchure on 28.1.1948, but he could not do so as Dr Parchure was very busy with Godse in discussion. I asked my source why Godse had gone to Dr. Parchure to which my source said that Godse was sent by Vir Savarkar of Bombay.[12]

Here the dots begin to connect. Between 8 August 1947 and 30 January 1948, there was one more meeting between Parchure and Savarkar, facilitated by none other than Karkare of Ahmednagar. Parchure told his interrogators later:

During November 1947 I had gone to Bombay to attend the Working Committee of the All India States Hindu Sabha ... At that time Kirkre [Karkare] stayed with me in the Kitte Bhandar Hall at Dadar. V.D. Savarkar's meeting was also arranged. After hearing my speech, Mr Kirkre invited me to come to Ahmednagar to address meetings.[13]

At 5.15 p.m. on 30 January 1948, Nathuram Godse killed Mahatma Gandhi.

For years, people have tried to find the 'smoking gun' linking Savarkar to the assassination, as he was acquitted in the Gandhi murder trial. The Jeevan Lal Kapur Commission report came close; the commission found that: 'All these facts taken together were destructive of any theory other than the conspiracy to murder by Savarkar and his group.'[14] But it still did not clinch matters. We believe the August conspiracy is the smoking gun everyone has been looking for.

2

The Accidental Breakthrough

4 February 1948, 2.30 p.m.

A tall, middle-aged cop, wearing a khaki turban and sporting a beard that looked like it had been painted on, was returning from the Safdarjung Aerodrome, the only airport in Delhi at the time. Deputy Superintendent of Police Sardar Jaswant Singh had just come back after dropping off a prized catch to the Bombay Police. The transfer was of Madanlal Pahwa, a refugee from Montgomery in Pakistan who had, on 20 January 1948, set off a guncotton slab in an attempt to kill Mahatma Gandhi.

DSP Singh's Ambassador car pulled over at the Tughlaq Road police station. He was tired; he hadn't slept in some days. Singh had spent twenty years in the police, most of them in Punjab. In 1945, he was transferred to Delhi as deputy superintendent of the Parliament Street area. The Parliament, the heart of a newly independent India's power in 1948, was a stone's throw away. Until four days ago, he thought he had seen it all—the imperialism of the British Raj, the rise and spread of the Indian freedom struggle, two world wars and India's tryst with destiny, bloodied by a violent partition. By now, Delhi had turned into a refugee capital. Truckloads of Sikhs and Hindus were arriving from Pakistan in what was one of the world's largest and most violent mass migrations in history. In 1947, Delhi was a city of almost one million people. More than three lakh Muslims left the city for Pakistan. At the same time, nearly five lakh non-Muslim refugees arrived into the capital from West Punjab, Sindh and the North West Frontier Province. Sixteen refugee camps came up in Delhi; the biggest was the one in front of Jama Masjid in north Delhi, as well as others in Nizamuddin, Okhla, and near Purana Quila and Humayun's Tomb in central Delhi. Refugees sought shelter everywhere—camps, mosques, temples, gurudwaras, schools, even graveyards.

People poured into Delhi carrying stories of unprecedented horror: of loved ones maimed, raped, butchered; of lifetimes of financial savings, assets, memories and lives left cruelly behind.

For a newly independent nation, a crisis of this magnitude and violence was baptism by fire. The city was a tinderbox and people's emotions were running high. The refugees were hungry, angry, cold and distrustful. The air was thick with fear, insecurity and plots of revenge. As waves of Partition violence washed over Hindus, Muslims and Sikhs, on 13 January 1948, a tired old fakir embarked upon his last satyagraha, vowing to end it only when 'peace has returned to Delhi ... when a Muslim can walk around in the city all by himself'[1] Mahatma Gandhi asked non-Muslim refugees not to occupy mosques or settle in Muslim neighbourhoods by force; he told every Hindu and Sikh not to touch a single Muslim; and he wanted the Indian government to release the balance of payments due to Pakistan, which amounted to 55 crore rupees.

At the time, there were many Hindu and Sikh refugees who wished Gandhi dead. Slogans like *'Gandhi ko marne do, hum ko ghar do'* rang out in the streets of Delhi.[2] On 20 January 1948, Madanlal Pahwa attempted to kill Gandhi and failed. Barely ten days later, on 30 January, Nathuram Godse fired three bullets that pierced the Mahatma's frail body. Newly independent India, still bleeding, wept and mourned.

DSP Jaswant Singh was put in charge of investigating Gandhi's murder.

30 January 1948

At around 5.30 p.m., DSP Singh was about to leave the Parliament Street police station when he received the news from the skeletal security detail posted at Gandhi's prayer meeting that Mahatma had been shot at. By the time he made his way to Birla House, about 6 kilometres away, Gandhi was lying in a pool of blood. He saw three wounds—one in the chest, one in the abdomen and a third in the stomach. All of them were on the right side of his body. One bullet was lodged in his chest, the other two had gone through his body. The white khaddar dhoti and woollen shawl that draped his frail frame were scorched by the bullets and bloodied. The seventy-eight-year-old satyagrahi had met a violent death.

If all had gone according to plan, Gandhi would have met his death a few days earlier, on 20 January. But Madanlal and his associates—Narayan Apte, Vishnu Karkare, Gopal Godse, Nathuram Godse, Dattatreya Parchure, Digambar Badge and Shankar Kistayya—couldn't pull it off. Perhaps it was destiny that that attempt had failed.

Since then, Madanlal was in DSP Singh's custody, after those gathered at the prayer meeting had caught him. Madanlal was a Punjabi refugee who had arrived in India in August 1947, at the height of Partition. He had lost his aunt to its brutal violence. He was deeply angry and dissatisfied with the pro-Muslim policies of Mahatma Gandhi at the time. In fact, he was so eager to see Gandhi dead that he confided in his benefactor in Bombay, Dr Jagdish Chandra Jain, about the conspiracy to murder the Father of the Nation before making the attempt.

There were various attempts made on Gandhi's life, but nobody came as close as Madanlal did. It was an audacious plan. He was to set off a bomb at Mahatma Gandhi's prayer meeting in Birla House to create confusion and one of his other associates was to take a shot at Gandhi in the ensuing chaos. However, it would appear that the squad left the prayer meeting before the bomb exploded. Madanlal was apprehended by the police and subjected to custodial torture. In a cruel twist of fate, Madanlal endured brutal third-degree punishment until he revealed their murderous plot to kill the messiah of truth and non-violence.

Madanlal gave up information on the conspiracy, but not so much about his co-conspirators. It was strange, but the truth was that he didn't know his assassination squad well. Seven decades later, can we really know if the information Madanlal provided would have been enough to stop Gandhi's assassination?

When DSP Singh began his investigation into Gandhi's murder, a lot was already known to the Delhi Police. By 26 January, four days before the successful assassination attempt, they had pieced together quite a bit of information on the conspiracy. A secret note of the Delhi Police from that day reveals that the police managed to extract just one name from Madanlal—that of his primary contact, Vishnu Ramkrishna Karkare, owner of the Deccan Guest House in the Kapada Bazar area of Ahmednagar, Maharashtra.

Vishnu Karkare was secretary of the Hindu Mahasabha in Ahmednagar since 1938. An orphan, Karkare had a difficult childhood. He ran away from his orphanage in Bombay to begin life anew in Poona by selling tea. Soon, he had a small tea stall in Ahmednagar, where he began to put down roots. Later, he opened a budget hotel. As his business prospered, he became a patron of theatre and the performing arts in Ahmednagar, acquiring social capital with the life he had built in the town. In 1938, he was elected unopposed to the town council and became secretary of the Hindu Mahasabha.

In November 1947, Madanlal Pahwa walked into his office.

*

During his police interrogation, Madanlal merely identified the rest of the squad as 'Marathas'. He told the police that seven people were directly involved in the plot and thirteen other people and places were connected to it tangentially, including Karkare and the Hindu Mahasabha Bhawan, situated near Gole Market in north-central Delhi.[3]

On 31 January, at the icy crack of dawn, 5.30 a.m., DSP Singh began his investigation into Gandhi's murder. The post-mortem report, prepared by Colonel B.L. Taneja at the Irwin Hospital, said that Gandhi had died of shock and internal hemorrhage from the gun wounds. Before the end of the day, the police had reached the doors of Hindu Mahasabha Bhawan, as identified by Madanlal.[4]

Nathuram Godse, the man who had fired the gun, was one of the seven 'Marathas' directly involved in the assassination, as per Madanlal's confession. Unaware of his name, Madanlal could only describe Godse as the 'proprietor of the *Hindu Rashtra*' in Poona. In reality, as described earlier, Godse was the editor of the rabidly right-wing Marathi newspaper *Dainik Agrani*, as *Hindu Rashtra* used to be called earlier.

All evidence so far pointed to Maharashtra as the cradle where the conspiracy must have been conceived.

DSP Singh met Godse for the first time on 30 January 1948 at around 7.15 p.m. in the Parliament Street police station. Godse had two minor wounds on his head and his cheek was bruised. He didn't say much, except to confess to the crime. The police had unwillingly seen the futility of subjecting him to torture; the murderer had confessed and the victim was beyond saving. However, a parade of the nation's who's who had arrived at Birla House, demanding answers to this heinous crime, from Viceroy Lord Mountbatten to independent India's first prime minister, Jawaharlal Nehru, and Home Minister Sardar Vallabhbhai Patel.

After the failed assassination attempt on 20 January, the police had begun the process of identifying a few of the 'Marathas' Madanlal had referred to. They now knew that the twenty-two-year-old young man Madanlal mentioned was Narayan Apte, publisher of Godse's paper, the *Dainik Agrani*. He joined the list of people to plot the most sensational assassination in contemporary history.

Gopal Godse was also one of the seven 'Marathas' identified by Madanlal. Gopal idolized his brother, Nathuram. A family man working at a transport company in Kirkee, Maharashtra, Gopal had served in the British Indian army's motor division and in Iraq and Iran during the Anglo-Iraqi war. On 17 January 1948, Gopal requested a week's leave from his supervisor, Leslie Bernard. He reported back to work on 26 January. Madanlal identified him as the 'brother of Proprietor [of *Hindu Rashtra*]'. Gopal couldn't match his brother's fervour for the plot to assassinate Gandhi but he lived to tell their tale.

Among the seven 'Marathas' there was also an 'owner–servant' pair—the 'owner of Poona's Shastra Bhandar', Digambar Badge, and his 'servant', Shankar Kistayya. In his interrogation, Madanlal also mentioned a priest from the 'Vishnu Bhagwan temple' in Bombay. Digambar Badge was a key figure in the investigation into Gandhi's murder; six months later, he would turn approver and testify against his co-conspirators. We know today that he did so at great personal risk. A top-secret report of the Intelligence Bureau dated 20 July 1948 showed that the RSS, or the Sangh 'has decided to murder the approver in Mahatma Gandhi's murder case'.[5] This was cited as a reason not to lift the ban on the RSS in July 1948.

4 February 1948

From this day on, events began to unfold fast and furious. The Indian government, still reeling from the shock of the Mahatma's assassination, decided to ban the RSS and was planning to make a big arrest—that of the prolific right-wing militant Hindu leader, Vinayak Damodar Savarkar.

Although the government was preparing to ban the RSS, there was no actual evidence at the time linking the organization to Gandhi's assassination. Out of the seven raids conducted by the Delhi Police in search of Gandhi's assassin, only one of them was on an RSS leader. The 2 February raid was on then municipal commissioner and RSS chalak (branch head) Hari Chand, where the police only recovered postcards, articles, some propaganda literature and a few paper cuttings on the basis of a First Information Report (FIR) filed at the Faiz Bazar police station.[6] Hauz Qazi Station House Officer Ram Dutt recovered eighteen documents from Hari Chand's residence, none of them incriminated the RSS.

But it was no secret that RSS had wished for Gandhi's death. In many meetings, its members had discussed Gandhi at length.

The Mahatma was the single-biggest stumbling block for the RSS and other like-minded militant Hindu organizations and their anti-Muslim agenda. In fact, the Crime Investigation Division of the Delhi Police and Intelligence Bureau had many intelligence reports to this effect.

Yet, on the day the RSS was banned, there wasn't a shred of evidence linking the organization to the murder. The Indian government was mistaken, particularly Home Minister Sardar Patel, in assuming that the RSS was a volunteering arm of the Hindu Mahasabha. In its formative years, the camaraderie between the Sangh and the Hindu Mahasabha gave an impression that both organizations were closely related. One of the two key strategies used by Hedgewar was to get a prominent Hindu Mahasabha member to host an RSS pracharak (worker) and introduce him to their areas and potential members, which only strengthened the belief that the two organizations worked closely. However, by the 1940s, the connection between the Sangh and Mahasabha was tenuous. They may have been ideologically aligned, but organizationally, the two had grown far apart.

It was a strange coincidence that the reason for their strained relationship was Vinayak Damodar Savarkar. In 1937, when Savarkar was elected president of the All India Hindu Mahasabha, he turned it into a political organization. This transformation ensured that whatever support the Sangh had rendered to the Mahasabha would cease. When the Second World War broke out, the RSS was concerned about a Japanese invasion of the subcontinent and preoccupied with post-war scenarios. It didn't want to invite the attention or the ire of the

British Indian government; it had to survive in order to defend Hindus, for which its strategy was to scrupulously avoid any political activity and help to the Hindu Mahasabha.

The strategy worked; the RSS survived. In 1943, three years after the ordinance banning military drills and uniforms came into effect, the British Indian government prepared a detailed dossier on whether they should proceed with more action against the Sangh. They concluded that 'it would be difficult to argue that the RSS constitutes an immediate menace to law and order'.[7]

A change in leadership in both organizations happened simultaneously. Savarkar took charge of the Mahasabha in 1937 and M.S. Golwalkar succeeded the more militant K.B. Hedgewar at the RSS in 1940. This was also the time when their approaches began to differ. Savarkar placed military training as top priority while Golwalkar wanted to abolish the military department of the RSS altogether.

However, the lack of evidence didn't stop the Indian government from arresting Golwalkar on 3 February 1948. On the other hand, DSP Singh had gathered a lot more direct evidence against Savarkar.

The 26 January interrogation report of Madanlal mentioned Savarkar. More than one needle of suspicion pointed towards Savarkar as the mastermind of the murder— partly because of his profile and also because of the low-key profiles of the co-consipirators. Far away from the chaos that had engulfed Delhi, Savarkar, ailing and retired from active politics, was in Bombay. Even in retirement, he was the tallest Hindutva leader.

The Green Taxi

DSP Singh interrogated Godse for the first time on the afternoon of 1 February 1948. The next day, the interrogation began at 10 a.m. and went on for nine hours until 7 p.m. On the third consecutive day, questioning began at around 1 p.m. So far, Godse had not cracked. He stuck to the story that he had masterminded the assassination, only conceding that he arrived in Delhi with Narayan Apte. The DSP had not managed to get any evidence confirming Savarkar's role. Frustrated, the cop noted, 'I continued interrogating Godse accused at Parliamentary Street police station, but nothing useful was revealed.'[8]

Time was moving. The pressure was building on DSP Singh to unravel the conspiracy. On 4 February at 5 p.m., the cop asked Head Constable Parasram to get a taxi for him. India, a young nation, was in dire need of resources; there weren't enough police vehicles to deploy, even for the country's most important investigation. It was at this time that destiny intervened once again.

The first taxi Parasram hailed was out of order. A second one came along, owned by Surjit Singh, a Jat driver from DSP Singh's native Jalandhar in Punjab. The cop recognized the taxi by its colour and number plate, 'PBF 671'; it was only two days ago that he had asked Assistant Sub-Inspector Shiv Prasad to trace this particular vehicle. One of the few details Godse had coughed up during interrogation was that he, Apte, Gopal and Karkare had left Birla House on 20 January in a green car chauffeured by a young Sikh driver, Surjit Singh.

Twenty-four-year-old Singh was the owner of a Chevrolet car, which was registered in Lahore. He had arrived in Delhi just six months ago and had been privately plying his car as a taxi. This was a second-hand car with very distinctive features that made it immediately noticeable in Delhi. For one, the colour of his car was green, the same as moong dal. His was perhaps the only car in the city at the time to have a luggage carrier; witnesses later identified this as the 'moongiya' car with the 'jungla' (luggage carrier) on top.

In a stroke of extraordinary luck, Parasram had hailed the same taxi that Godse and the others used as a getaway vehicle after the first assassination attempt.

Rewind

On 20 January, Surjit Singh's green taxi had picked up four passengers from the Regal Cinema taxi stand. Their destination was Birla House, via Birla Mandir, located on Albuquerque Road (now Tees January Marg). His four passengers were Narayan Apte, Digambar Badge, Shankar Kistayya and Gopal Godse. This hardly raised any suspicion; after all, people often came to attend Gandhi's evening prayer meetings. The car was parked at the back of Birla House. The four passengers entered and made their way to the servant quarters.

Surjit Singh himself entered the prayer ground and waited for about fifteen minutes. Prayers had not yet begun and the loudspeaker seemed to be out of order. Forty-five minutes after disembarking, the passengers returned. However, Badge did not return. Nathuram Godse came instead. As they sat in the car, an explosion went off inside Birla House. The passengers asked Surjit Singh to 'start the car' twice.

The cabbie's account showed that the four members of Gandhi's murder squad left the scene of crime before Madanlal ignited the guncotton. Badge and his servant were still at the prayer meeting, while Madanlal was apprehended by an enraged crowd after a witness, Sulochana Devi, pointed him out to the constables guarding the house.

Sulochana Devi was in her early twenties. She lived about 200 to 300 steps from the Birla House at 9, Albuquerque Road. In her account, she said she was following her three-year-old child who had run out of the house towards Birla House from the back. She had seen a 'moongiya coloured' car parked there. Nearly fifteen paces from her, she saw Madanlal placing a bomb and lighting a matchstick to ignite it. Then the explosion happened.

Surjit Singh dropped off the murder squad at Tata Airways in Connaught Place. Just a few hours earlier, the group had united for one last time at Room Number 40 of Marina Hotel, also in Connaught Place, where they stayed until 4 p.m. that day. This was the same hotel Apte and Godse had checked into a few days earlier, on 17 January, under the false names of S. Deshpande and M. Deshpande. Gobindram, a twenty-year-old bearer at the Marina Hotel, even reported that the people in Room Number 40 ordered one peg of whiskey the first day and two pegs the next day. All drinks were consumed by Karkare, the sethji.

At 4 p.m. on 20 January, Godse left for Birla House on a tonga owned by Munshi Ram, whereas four others took Surjit

Singh's green taxi. On that morning, the squad met at the Hindu Mahasabha Bhawan. The jungle behind the building served as a shooting range for Gopal Godse to practise firing with his revolver. Madanlal borrowed a screwdriver and some oil from the Hindu Mahasabha Bhawan to tinker with the revolver. Nathuram Godse was not present as he was unwell.

Madanlal and Karkare took a tonga back to the hotel for the final meeting. The squad went over the plan; Apte would show them the place where Madanlal was to set off the bomb; Badge would throw a hand grenade through a ventilator; and in the ensuing chaos, Gopal would shoot Gandhi. Each of them would position themselves strategically at Birla House. On the day of the shooting, Madanlal, Godse, Badge and Karkare were in position at the prayer meeting, while Apte and Gopal waited near the taxi. Madanlal set off the bomb between 4 and 4.30 p.m., but the rest of the plan fell through disastrously.

At Tata Airways, where Surjit Singh's taxi had dropped them, the squad parted ways. Gopal left for Hindu Mahasabha Bhawan, where he was instructed to leave for Poona; Godse and Apte made their way to the New Delhi Railway Station. Karkare went back to Marina Hotel to retrieve some clothes he had given to wash, after which he too reported to the Hindu Mahasabha Bhawan. But the others had already left the building. By 21 January, the squad had dispersed.

Between 31 January and 1 February, after making arrangements for Gandhi's funeral, the Delhi Police raided the Hindu Mahasabha Bhawan at midnight. DSP Singh's crackdown began at what appeared to be the headquarters of the conspiracy to murder Gandhi—the Hindu Mahasabha Bhawan.

To Jaswant Singh, the Hindu Mahasabha was fast emerging as the epicentre of Gandhi's assassination. Founded in 1915, the organization initially advocated Hindu–Muslim unity. The Mahasabha traces its origin to the Punjab Hindu Sabha established in 1908–09, where Bhai Paramanand planted the seeds of Hindutva politics. Its philosophical moorings were largely derived from two written works, *Our Earliest Attempts at Independence* by Bhai Parmanand and *The Indian War of Independence 1857* by Vinayak Damodar Savarkar. Both works, written in 1909, were romanticized accounts of the 1857 Indian Mutiny and Hindu–Muslim unity. In the beginning, the organization searched for this elusive and perhaps imaginary unity. By 1920, however, things shifted fundamentally. The Hindu Mahasabha transformed itself into a militant force for protecting the interest of Hindus alone. Savarkar defined Hindus as all those who loved the land that stretched from the Sindhu River in the west to the seas in the east. The ideal Hindu must look upon India not only as his fatherland, but his holy land as well.

After the First World War, the world order underwent a serious change. The break-up of the Ottoman Empire at the hands of British forces created a backlash among Indian Muslims, who put up a united front against the British that eventually took the form of the Khilafat Movement in 1919, which garnered Gandhi and the Indian National Congress's unwavering support. The idea behind their backing of the Khilafat agitation was to present a unified Hindu–Muslim front to the British. But hardliners such as Savarkar and Hedgewar began to feel that this support was going too far. Around this time, the Hindu Mahasabha had already begun to abandon its ideas of Hindu–Muslim unity.

In 1921, the Moplah Rebellion took place in Malabar, Kerala. This uprising was inspired by the Khilafat Movement; however, it turned violent. When it began, the revolt was against the British, but soon the Muslim peasants turned their attention towards the landed Hindu elite in the region. A section of the Muslim peasantry unleashed violence against the repressive Hindu zamindars, raping women and pillaging and burning their houses. This chain of events wrought a crucial change in Savarkar's attitude towards Hindu–Muslim unity. He moved towards strengthening and uniting Hindus, the blueprint for which he laid down in his 1923 book *Essentials of Hindutva*.

On 20 August 1923, the members of the Hindu Mahasabha met in Benares (now Varanasi), bringing together the various warring factions of Hindus under one roof. Their primary focus was to urgently establish a united Hindu front in the face of Indian Muslim unity, which had successfully shown itself in the Khilafat and Moplah agitations.

Simultaneously, a major social reformation was afoot in British India. In some parts of the country, there was a growing anti-Brahmin movement and opposition towards the urban-based commercial and professional classes. As a result of two British reform movements—the Morley–Minto Reforms in 1909 and the Montagu–Chelmsford Reforms in 1918—the government increasingly favoured rural areas at the expense of urban regions that gave rise to a rich and vocal peasant lobby. By the mid 1920s, political and social changes made it imperative for the affluent, urban commercial and professional Hindus to organize themselves against forces that were undermining their power and position.

It would seem that class identity had begun to merge along religious lines and the threat to the upper classes was met by the strengthening of religious identity. In Maharashtra, the urban Brahmins had begun to face pushback from the Kunbi Maratha castes—peasants who had benefited from the British reforms. Similarly, in Punjab in 1921–23, Fazl-i-Husain, the founder of the Unionist Party of Punjab whose members comprised Jat Sikhs and other non-Brahmin Hindu castes, launched an attack on rich, landowning upper-caste Hindus.[9] The Moplah rebellion of 1921 was also an attack of the peasantry on rich, upper-caste landowning Hindus. To the Hindu Mahasabha-ites, these peasant caste-led attacks on upper castes stemmed from a single cause—the weakness and disunity among Hindus as a whole. Therefore, Savarkar's efforts towards uniting all Hindus revolved around stressing the cultural definition of the word 'Hindu' and the common racial history of all castes.

Despite these efforts, for most of its existence, the Hindu Mahasabha never became a mass organization as many of its supporters were rich landlords who were unwilling to allow even a whisper of mobilization. It remained a loosely organized group centred around prominent individuals.

To DSP Singh, the centrality of the Hindu Mahasabha to the murder plot made ample sense. In the eighteen raids his team had conducted till then, nearly all suspects were affluent businessmen or upper-caste Hindus wielding disproportionate power. Savarkar was a natural suspect, going by Madanlal's statement, Savarkar's track record of virulent Hinduism and his very public opposition to Mahatma Gandhi.

On 5 February, the Bombay Police detained Vinayak Damodar Savarkar.

3

The Recruit

August 1947

MADANLAL Pahwa's life was about to be upended. On 9 August, British lawyer and civil servant Cyril John Radcliffe submitted a border he had drawn, dividing the subcontinent along religious lines. Muslim-majority provinces in the north of India, west Punjab and east Bengal would become part of the new nation of Pakistan; Hindu and Sikh provinces would join India. Radcliffe, who had only arrived in India in July, was given a little over a month to equitably carve up 450,000 square kilometres of territory and decide the fate of eighty-eight million people. Up until 17 August, two days after Independence, people on both sides of the border had little clue where they would belong. The land was enveloped in an air of disbelief and denial, both before and after Partition. An advisor to the Punjab Boundary Commission did not believe that an actual mass transfer of population would occur, while a family in Delhi was certain the city would go to Pakistan.[1]

Madanlal Kashmirilal Pahwa was twenty years old at the time. He was a resident of Pakpattan, a small town in Montgomery district in the Punjab province, where his family owned four marabbas (around 40 hectares) of land. His father Kashmirilal was a clerk in the settlement office; his mother died when Madanlal was just twenty days old. In 1947, he had returned home after two years of military service, before which he had served in the Navy as a wireless telegrapher. Madanlal had planned to sit for the Prabhakar examination[2], but it was not to be. 'I was not destined for the life of an ordinary peaceful, useful citizen,' Madanlal later said.[3] His testimony, despite the 'occasional exaggerations and propaganda',[4] too reveals the story of a Hindu refugee who witnessed first-hand violence that was ruthless and unsparing. To him, the Partition was a 'holocaust'.

In March 1947, the Khizar Hayat Tiwana ministry governing the Punjab province resigned, making way for the Muslim League. Communal riots erupted in Lahore and Amritsar and spread across Punjab.[5] It became clear to young Madanlal and many like him that the 'Hindu' leadership had completely failed and a partition was imminent. 'Fear and alarm seized Hindu Punjab,' Madanlal recalled.[6] Organized attempts were made to hoist the Muslim League flag on the Government House in Punjab, while 'the biggest of

League leaders' joined illegal and violent processions and demonstrations, according to him. The Muslim offensive, Madanlal told the court, was launched on the day of Holi when the Hindu procession in Pakpattan was stopped. '[The] Goondaism that is inherent in the Muslim nature came out in all its hideous ugliness.'[7]

On the evening of 3 June 1947, Lord Mountbatten, Jawaharlal Nehru, Muhammad Ali Jinnah and Baldev Singh sat in a hot studio in the imperial capital of Delhi and announced the plan for Partition. From Quetta to Madras, Calcutta to Bombay, people gathered around radios and wireless sets wherever they could to hear the news.[8] It came as a cruel shock to Madanlal, who felt betrayed and angry with his leaders for apportioning most of Punjab to Pakistan. He said that the whole of Hindu Punjab felt deceived and helpless. Their protests went unheard. The predominantly Muslim police force in the region shot at them and arrested them. Leaders who had accepted the Radcliffe Line promised to protect the interests of the Hindus in Punjab and advised them to stay put. Congress members even abused the people who tried to migrate at the time. On the other hand, Madanlal recalled, Muslims were preparing for Pakistan. Hindu houses were searched and even their kitchen knives were taken away. Muslim League flags were hoisted in towns and villages, and Hindus and Sikhs were asked to salute them.

Sometime later, in the month of August, the Muslim inflow from India began to arrive in special trains, which had the Muslim League flag flying atop and 'Pakistan Zindabad' painted on them. Word went around in Pakpattan that such a special train was expected on 19 August 1947. On 20 August, riots broke out. According to Madanlal, the Dogra Regiment arrived in Pakpattan on 23 August and, under their protection, a caravan of sixty thousand people began to march towards the town of Fazilka in the Indian state of Punjab. With almost no notice, Madanlal, like many other Hindus and Sikhs, hurriedly prepared to flee east in the face of impending violence, barbarity and death. It was a long trek of more than 100 kilometres. For three days and three nights, men, women and children of all ages and conditions marched with nothing more than the clothes on their back. The caravan was attacked many times. Many people—mostly women and children— could not take the strain and were left behind. Men were killed and women abducted.

When Madanlal and the remaining members finally arrived in Fazilka, they let out a collective cry of joy at the sight of Indian soil, hoping for some peace and safety. However, that was not the case. While some parts of Delhi were erupting in celebrations, Fazilka was under strict curfew. Soldiers of the Madras Regiment were on patrol, shooting at any civilian violating the curfew. The next day, Madanlal was reunited with a few of his relatives at a dharmashala for refugees. He received information that his father and aunt were arriving in a train from Pakpattan. A little later, he heard that the train was attacked. A few hundred people were killed, including his aunt. Madanlal felt this loss deeply, for she had raised him like her own son. Madanlal's father Kashmirilal was found wounded, lying in a heap of dead bodies. He was taken to the Ferozepur Cantonment hospital.

Due to his service record, Madanlal was drafted as a volunteer to transport and receive refugees. On 29 August, he heard about the arrival of a caravan of one lakh refugees, which was 60 kilometres long. The caravan included 500 women who had been stripped naked. 'I saw women with their breasts, noses, ears and cheeks cut ... I was told ghastly stories of devilish treatment. One told me the story of how her child was roasted and she was asked to partake of the same and on her refusal her ears were cut. Another told me how she was ravished in the presence of her husband who was tied to a tree.'[9]

By the end of August, communal violence had spread to Fazilka. Some Muslims had taken over the 'kassab mohalla' (butcher's colony) in the town, and a Hindu refugee was killed there. The police could not go into the area, nor did they allow the passage of a Gandhian official who had ensured the safe passage of Muslims just a few days before. Madanlal later recalled that this official had apologized to the Muslims before they were sent away in lorries and trucks to Pakistan. Despite this, the 'Muslim kassabs' of Fazilka refused to yield. They opened fire and the police returned it. On the outskirts of the town, refugees had come under attack again. Madanlal accompanied the police to those areas, where they found a large number of corpses and several refugees badly injured. He found a gravely wounded Sikh whose wife told him that her daughters had been abducted in Chak Bedi (now in Pakistan).

Madanlal then left for Ferozepur to reunite with his father. The town was under curfew, so he spent the night at the railway station. When a special train arrived from Rawalpindi in Pakistan, Madanlal talked to a few passengers onboard, who also told him harrowing tales about the mass slaughter that was carried out in Raiwind on a special train ferrying 2,500 passengers. Later, he visited his father at the cantonment hospital. Kashmirilal was weak and covered in bandages, yet he urged his son to leave for Delhi as soon as possible. It was a traumatic time for young Madanlal, as it was for the fifteen million people who were displaced, dispossessed, robbed, injured, killed and raped. Whole villages were set aflame; men, women and children were hacked to death; young women were raped; and pregnant women had their breasts cut off. There was slaughter everywhere.

Madanlal reached Delhi via Bhatinda and Ambala, and headed for the refugee camp. Later, he moved to his maternal aunt's place in Gwalior, Madhya Pradesh, where he worked with Dattatreya Sadashiv Parchure's militant organization called Hindu Rashtra Sena—a key figure in the conspiracy to murder Mahatma Gandhi. In Gwalior, Madanlal was part of a gang that attacked Muslims on the streets of the city. The same gang also attacked a train ferrying Muslims from Gwalior to Bhopal with pistols and hand grenades.[10]

After he came to India, Madanlal was in need of a job. His father Kashmirilal had wanted him to find a job in Delhi; he wrote a chit to his brother-in-law to take Madanlal to a police officer for a job as a constable. Madanlal did not want to become a constable but he did not want to admit that to his father, so he kept the chit with him.

In Gwalior, for twenty days, he looked for jobs but could not secure anything. On his aunt's advice he remained near the railway station in search of a job for two days. Once again he was unsuccessful.

Rebuilding His Life

Two months after the independence of India, in October, Madanlal moved to Bombay without telling his aunt. He had been to Bombay and Poona earlier. In November 1944, as a seventeen-year-old, he had joined the Royal Indian Engineers (RIE) in Lahore, like other middle-class boys who aspired for secure jobs in imperial institutions. After completing his training at Nawroz Ji Wadia College in Poona, he was posted in Bombay with the British Indian Royal Navy.

On the train from Gwalior to Bombay, Madanlal travelled along with many other Hindu refugees making their passage to safer ports in the hope of restarting their violently uprooted lives. The train carriages reeked of spilt blood and dead bodies; people swapped horrifying stories of irreparable loss and savage inhumanity.

Madanlal was mad with rage; he found solace among his community of exiled Hindus. Human beings can only process a limited amount of change in a short period of time without experiencing anxiety. When rapid and tragic change occurs in a society, with ethno-nationalism based on religion, geography or ethnicity at its nucleus, then the definition of who qualifies as a full member of that society narrows down. This process is called 'othering'. It was not surprising, then, that hundreds of Hindus and Sikhs like Madanlal in India and Muslims in

Pakistan felt unbridled anger and hatred towards members of other communities who had once been their neighbours.

On the Bombay-bound train, Madanlal and his fellow Hindu refugees longed to throw Muslim travellers off it. The stories of brutality they had heard and exchanged, the violence they had witnessed and suffered, the loved ones they had lost, enraged and overwhelmed them. For Madanlal, it was 'us Hindus' versus 'those Muslims'.

October 1947

Bombay was in the throes of chaos. Trains and ships packed with refugees were arriving in the city with unceasing regularity; scores of makeshift camps had sprung up; and gurudwaras were arranging hot meals for the refugees. While Punjabi refugees boarded the Frontier Mail, renowned for its speed and punctuality, at Peshawar, non-Muslims from Sindh climbed the train at Hasan Abdal and made their way to Bombay over three days and 2,335 kilometres. Others like Madanlal who had left west Punjab earlier for other cities in India also made their way to Bombay. Some refugees also took the shorter and safer sea route to Bombay from Karachi, a mere 589 nautical miles away. The first refugee camps in Bombay came up in Sion-Koliwada, Queens Road, Frere Road and Ridley's Siding, which later became Ulhasnagar.

For the first few days, Madanlal took refuge in a gurdwara in the Bori Bunder area. The gurdwara helped him with a square meal and a place to sleep. It was no solution to his miseries and the Indian bureaucracy, overwhelmed by its work, did not make it easy for him either. He went to the Pulton Road police station to get an identification card. Those days a refugee needed an identity card. Madanlal registered with the police station and was given an identity—No. 153. The next stop was the refugee commissioner's office for a job. Refugees had been pouring into Bombay, which was one of the few prosperous cities in the subcontinent. The refugee commissioner's office asked him to go to the Punjab and Frontier Association and fill up a form. Form in hand, he went to Sharma Electric Stores in Crawford Market. The form was signed by the shopkeeper who kept a counterfoil and returned the rest of the form to Madanlal. He had to go back with this countersigned form to the commissioner's office to get a place in the Chembur refugee camp, as he could only stay for three days in the gurdwara. Madanlal moved to Barrack No. T-162 of the camp, which housed eighty other bachelor refugees. Political workers from the Indian National Congress, Communist Party and the Hindu Mahasabha visited the camps, offered support and made lofty promises to rebuild the lives of these displaced and dispossessed men.

Every morning, Madanlal would 'set off for the city and tramp its steamy streets in search of a job. He did not make a good, docile refugee.'[11] Thickset and muscular with dark brown hair, Madanlal wore a permanent scowl on his face. At the Chembur camp, he made some friends, along with whom he began to kill Muslims in the city.

If it was the death of humanity that engulfed Madanlal's life, it was also the touch of humanity that gave refugees like him some hope. At the refugee camp, he heard that Prithviraj, an actor, was giving money to the refugees at Opera House cinema. He went there and stood in a queue of fifty to sixty refugees for the eight rupees that Prithviraj himself handed out.

In October 1947, Madanlal met Dr Jagdish Chandra Jain, a professor of Ardhamagadhi and Hindi at Ramnarain Ruia College in Bombay. Dr Jain offered the young refugee a job as a book salesperson. For the next couple of days, Madanlal visited the professor daily and sold his books in Bombay. In about ten days Madanlal earned fifty rupees.[12] At the time, he was also in the 'firecracker business.' In fact, he had to chop off the top of the index finger of his left hand when it got caught in a machine at the illegal firecracker factory.

Later, he met J.S. Sud, a refugee from Lahore, and together they came up with a plan to sell fruit—mosambis—that they would source cheaply from Ahmednagar. Madanlal was lucky to have made it to India alive through the Partition violence. However, his life as a refugee was no less harrowing than the journey he undertook.

In early November, Madanlal and J.S. Sud left for Ahmednagar on a passenger train, armed with savings of fifty rupees and eighty books and 300 balloons to sell on the way. Before leaving, they bought mosambis worth thirty-six rupees. It was Muharram, the start of the new year according to the Islamic calendar. Ahmednagar was mostly shut.

Madanlal had walked into a city that was a potential tinderbox. Ahmednagar shared its border with the state of Hyderabad, where the Razakars were locked in a violent battle with workers of the Hyderabad State Congress. At the time of

Madanlal's visit, plans by the State Congress in collaboration with some Mahasabhaites were afoot to blow up the four bridges that connected Ahmednagar to Hyderabad.

Even seven centuries ago, the region used to be a regular battleground for Hindu kingdoms and Muslim conquerors. Ahmednagar, named after the founder of the Nizam Shahi dynasty, Ahmad Nizam Shah, creaked under the weight of 700 years of tumultuous history. In 1296, Alauddin Khilji led the first Muslim incursion into the Deccan, when he raided Devagiri, the capital of the Yadava dynasty, situated just over 100 km from Ahmednagar. Khilji used the wealth looted from here to stage a coup d'etat on the Delhi Sultanate and overthrow his uncle, Jalaluddin. For the next 400 years until 1759, Ahmednagar remained the seat of Muslim rulers of the Bahmani, Nizam Shahi and then the Mughal dynasties. Towards the end of the seventeenth century and the beginning of the eighteenth, the Mughals, under Aurangzeb, were locked in constant battle with the Maratha kingdom. Aurangzeb died in Ahmednagar in 1707, amidst a succession of wars with the Marathas to claim the Deccan that led to the eventual decline of the Mughal empire, the short-lived expansion of the Maratha kingdom into the North and the Northwest, and the advent of the colonial British empire.

The city had borne witness to power tussles, invasions, plots and violence over centuries between militant Hindu warriors and Muslim rulers. By 1947, Hindutva had made a permanent home here. The history of the Maratha army under Shivaji, Sambhaji and Rajaram, as they valiantly engaged the Muslim invader Aurangzeb's mighty forces in a decades-long battle, became an essential part of the narrative that was routinely used to motivate and forge a militant Hindu identity. It was here that Madanlal and Sud saw the board 'H.M.S. Office Veer Savarkar Watchanalai' (Hindu Mahasabha Office Veer Savarkar Reading Room), as they drove past in a tonga. Their interest piqued, the two refugees walked upstairs where Vishnu Karkare met them for the first time.

Sowing the Seeds

Vishnu Ramakrishna Karkare had a fair, cherubic face. Bespectacled, with a closely cropped beard, he usually wore a simple shirt, dhoti and a Gandhi topi. His benign looks, however, belied a permanently angry air about him. Life had dealt a cruel hand to Karkare from the time of his birth. Born into a Brahmin family, he lost his father when he was a baby. He grew up in the Northcote Orphanage in Bombay. With true grit, he acquired formidable social capital over decades. By 1947, Karkare, who had started out as a chaiwalla, was a prominent social worker, funding poor students and local theatre groups. He owned a boarding and lodging house called the Deccan Guest House in the city. He had also started the Ahmednagar branch of the Hindu Mahasabha.

This was not Madanlal's first run-in with the Hindu Mahasabha. He had met Dr Jain in Bombay through the Sabha, and he had worked with the HRS in Gwalior. Hoping that the Sabha connection would prove lucky again, Madanlal tried to enlist Karkare's help in selling Dr Jain's books in Ahmednagar. He also explained his plan of selling mosambis cheaply in

Bombay. This gave Karkare the idea to persuade Madanlal to set up a coconut stall instead in front of his boarding and lodging house.

Karkare's seemingly kind offer had an ulterior motive. Riots, history tells us, are often communal or sectarian in nature; however, the targets of such conflicts are usually economic. In the subcontinent, the complex nature of social formation based on caste, ethnicity and religion gives every economic activity a community identity. Karkare's offer to Madanlal had two motives—to help a refugee stand on his feet and, more importantly, to break the monopoly enjoyed by Muslims in the coconut trade in Ahmednagar.

So Madanlal, bankrolled by Karkare, went into the coconut trade, starting out with 100 coconuts, and free boarding and lodging at the Deccan Guest House.

A Willing Instrument

Almost a week into his coconut trade, Madanlal accompanied Karkare to the Visapur refugee camp, some 40 km away from Ahmednagar. Karkare arrived with a clear agenda—to instigate the refugees against the Muslim community in Ahmednagar. To this end, he called on them to enter the Muslim-dominated fruit trade. Madanlal was the first successful refugee fruit trader who had done just that.

Sindhi Hindu refugees came to the Visapur camp on special trains. They managed with the food, clothes and soap provided by the people of Ahmednagar. Sometime later, when this camp was shut down, the refugees moved to another camp in Kalyan,

Bombay. Proud Sindhis in Visapur like Laxmandas Makhija felt that the 'free facilities would not last forever and in any case, they could not live off them any more [sic]' so they began to look for employment.[13]

Karkare and Madanlal could not have arrived at the Visapur camp at a more opportune time. To the Sindhi refugees, whose lives had been abruptly uprooted, who had had to make excruciating journeys to reach safety and whose existential anxieties were very real, Karkare's proposal was a godsend. On the one hand, Mahatma Gandhi was trying to console a bleeding, severed nation through collective solidarity; on the other, in Ahmednagar, Karkare was exploiting people's anger, fears and insecurities.

Convinced, 500 refugees from the Visapur camp moved to Ahmednagar to restart life as fruit traders. They set up base in a municipal school and Karkare's hotel supplied food to them. However, there were initial hiccups—there were not enough places in the city for all the refugees to open fruit shops. Muslim traders were already present at the prime locations. Karkare came up with a crafty solution to this problem: the refugees were told to take out a procession to make the city aware of their circumstances and support their business ventures. Karkare even had the slogans ready—'*Nirwastoon ko dhandha do*' (Give refugees business); '*Humein bhi shehr me basao*' (Accommodate us also in the city); '*Jangalon me mat phenko*' (Do not throw us in the jungles); '*Hum campon ki rotiyan khana pasand nahi karte*' (We do not like the food being served in refugee camps).

Madanlal led the first such refugee procession in Ahmednagar from the municipal school where they were camped to the market area. He addressed the crowd that had gathered and demanded fruit shops for refugees. This protest march made so much noise that it came to the attention of the highest police officials in the district and the state, who agreed to some of their demands. The agreement was subsequently not honoured. To Madanlal and his fellow refugee protestors, this only reinforced the belief that the new Indian government was pro-Muslim and anti-Hindu.

Ten days after the first march, the refugees took out a second rally through the bazaar area and wound up outside Sarosh Cinema. This time, they directly demanded that Sarosh Irani, the owner of the cinema and of the private bus transport in the city, employ Hindu refugees as 50 per cent of his workforce. This meant that the already employed Muslims in his cinema and bus company would lose their jobs. Once again, the rehabilitation of refugees grabbed headlines in Ahmednagar, prompting law-and-order officials to intervene. A meeting was convened at the deputy commissioner's bungalow later that day where the city's prominent citizens were invited to carry out deliberations on the refugee rehabilitation crisis. Madanlal was representing the refugees. In less than a fortnight, he had led his first political agitation and managed to extract valuable concessions from the city for displaced Sindhi refugees. Sarosh Irani agreed to pay for the refugees' sustenance and the city promised to open a bank to fund refugee projects.

In his young life, bruised so bloodily by the Partition, Madanlal had not tasted victory like this previously. He had successfully led a brotherhood of refugees, his anger towards the Muslims had found a channel—he thought he had found his purpose. In less than six months since Independence and the partition of India, a twenty-year-old refugee had transformed into a Hindu radical who would soon meet other likeminded young Hindu men and plot and carry out the assassination of the Father of the Nation.

The Hindu Brotherhood

By December 1947, Madanlal, mentored by Karkare, had achieved some success for his fellow refugees. They had opened up fruit shops in Ahmednagar and received a host of benefits from the government. They had also kept up their political activity, engaging with issues facing the young, newly independent nation and talking to its leaders.

At the time, Kashmir was in the news. In October 1947, Pakistan backed raiders advancing into Kashmir, evoking a response from the Maharaja of Jammu and Kashmir, who sought India's assistance. By January 1948, the Kashmir issue made its debut at the UN, when India tabled it and Kashmir became a bilateral issue between India and Pakistan—a conflict that continues until today. On 5 January 1948, the Congress party office in Ahmednagar organized a public meeting on Kashmir. Raosaheb Patwardhan, a Congress leader, was to address the gathering, as he had just returned from the Valley. Madanlal and other refugees were in attendance. The Congress leader spoke echoed Jawaharlal Nehru's line that Sheikh Abdullah should be left in charge of Kashmir affairs.

Om Prakash Chopra, a twenty-two-year-old refugee from Lahore in the audience, sent a written request to Raosaheb on stage, seeking an opportunity for their 'leader' Madanlal to speak on the issue. The Congress veteran tore up the request. This triggered a protest from the refugees, who brought the meeting to an end. Madanlal and his friends Om Prakash and Prakash Chand Bhatia were detained in a police lock-up that night. They were let off only after the intervention of the deputy commissioner.

Later that night, Karkare visited the trio. Prakash Chand, a twenty-eight-year-old curly-haired, fair refugee from Lahore, was the oldest among the three. Om Prakash was twenty-two; Madanlal, their 'leader', was, as previously mentioned, only twenty years old. That night, Karkare revealed to the three young men a plan that would forever alter the course of history of a newly independent country and of the Hindu Mahasabha: a plot to assassinate Mahatma Gandhi. The Hindu Mahasabha wanted to bring Hindu Raj into India as soon as possible, but Gandhi was their biggest obstacle. For the Hindu Mahasabha to flourish, Gandhi had to go.[14] Before Karkare could even explain fully, Madanlal was in.

The next morning, 11 January 1948, Karkare, Madanlal, Prakash Chand and Om Prakash left for Poona to meet with the person who was behind this outrageous plot. Arriving in Poona at 6 a.m. on 12 January, they first took a bus, then walked some distance to get to the *Hindu Rashtra* newspaper office. So far, only Karkare knew the identity of the person they were about to meet. A fair-complexioned man, with a muffler tied around his neck that partially covered his face, sat in a tent next to the office. Without introducing himself, the man left the tent, asking the others to wait. Madanlal would never know his name, but he had just met Narayan Apte.

Many hours later, around 5 p.m., Apte returned to the tent with the information that the arms supplier to carry out their plot would arrive that night. Until then, Madanlal and the other refugees passed time at the cinema, watching the movie *Doosri Shaadi* starring Mumtaz Shanti, one of the earliest stars of Bombay cinema, who moved away to Pakistan with her filmmaker-husband Wali Saheb in the early 1950s.

Later that night, Karkare took the trio to the arms supplier's house in Poona. Digambar Badge, sporting a saffron turban over his long hair, sat in the living room, while the Hindu Mahasabha held its meeting in the adjoining room. Chewing on betel leaves, Badge asked his attendant to bring the weapons. Much of the conversation was in Marathi, which Madanlal did not entirely follow. Shankar Kistayya, the attendant, first brought a yellow cloth bag. Inside it were fifteen military-made hand grenades. One grenade was passed around the room in silence. Before stepping into Badge's home, Karkare had warned the trio to keep mum and ask no questions.

Ten minutes later, Kistayya returned with a white bag containing two explosive slabs, gun cotton and fuses. Badge took out a slab and fitted it with the detonator, cord and fuse. This was a crude explosive that was generally used to blow up bridges. It was the explosive that Madanlal would use on 20 January 1948 in an attempt to assassinate Gandhi. Ten more minutes later, Kistayya came out with a khaki bag, with a 12-bore gun in it. It barrel, with a coin-size diameter, was fitted to an iron butt; once assembled, the gun was about 1–2 metres long. A little later, the last set arrived—two small white-coloured bags, one carrying 400 to 500 .303 rifle bullets and revolver bullets of various kinds, and the other with twenty small pistols. Badge instructed the others that the pistols were only for close-range use.

With the weapons secured for the assassination plot, the next stop for Karkare and the boys was Bombay. At the Poona railway station, they ate at an Irani café before boarding the train. Karkare and Madanlal boarded the train to Bombay, while Prakash Chand and Om Prakash returned to the Visapur camp to pack a few clothes for the trip that had no return date. It was 13 January, and the group had not lost a single day since the plot was conceived and put into action.

The Last Stop

On 13 January 1948, at around 6 a.m., a train pulled in at the Dadar GIP station (the Great Indian Peninsula Railway, which was the predecessor to the Indian Central Railway). Karkare and Madanlal got off and headed towards Shivaji Park, less than 2 kilometres away. At Savarkar Sadan, the home of Vinayak Damodar Savarkar where he spent three decades until his death in 1966, Karkare and Madanlal waited for a 'darshan' of the tallest Hindu Mahasabha leader. Four hours later, Savarkar met with them. Madanlal was overwhelmed and kept silent throughout the exchange, which took place in Marathi. In August 1947, an arbitrary line had butchered a land into two and left millions of lives like his in uncertainty.

Less than six months later, he found himself in the thick of things—a radicalized foot soldier in Savarkar's audacious plan for a Hindu Raj in a newly independent secular Gandhian India.

The next stage of the operation unfolded in Bombay and Ahmednagar over three to four days. In dire need of a change of clothes, Madanlal borrowed four rupees from Karkare to return to Ahmednagar. Travelling ticketless (since refugees were allowed to do so), Madanlal left Bombay at 2 p.m. on 13 January and reached Ahmednagar seven hours later. First, he handed over a letter addressed to Karkare's wife, written in Marathi, and then went to sleep in the Hindu Mahasabha office premises. He met Om Prakash and Prakash Chand at the Deccan Guest House for breakfast, packed his clothes and collected Karkare's bag. With a ten-rupee loan from Karkare's wife, the trio climbed on to a Bombay-bound train at midnight.

Their train pulled into Dadar GIP at noon the next day. When they made their way to the Hindu Mahasabha Office, the secretary, a namesake of the leader Savarkar, greeted them and arranged for their meals. Madanlal recognized him; the secretary had visited him at the Chembur refugee camp and helped him find a job. A short while later, Madanlal was back at his old quarters—Barrack No. T-162, Chembur camp—where he incited the refugees to take out a procession against the government.

Over the next two days, Madanlal and his fellow refugees waited for instructions from Karkare. While Madanlal missed a few meetings with Karkare, Om Prakash and Prakash Chand visited some old friends. They also went to the cinema to watch *Wamaq Azra*, starring Swarn Lata and Nazim Ahmed Khan, who also later got married and moved to Pakistan.

On 16 January 1948, the main conspirators of the assassination of Mahatma Gandhi gathered at the Hindu Mahasabha office in Dadar. Three people in the room were familiar to Madanlal—arms supplier Digambar Badge, the Hindu Mahasabhite from Poona Narayan Apte and Badge's helper Shankar Kistayya. There were two more men present in the room that day, Nathuram Godse and his brother Gopal Godse. After the meeting, the Godses left with Apte in a taxi. Karkare left too. Badge and Kistayya left early next morning.

The Maharashtrians took no notice of Madanlal. To them he was just a foot soldier. The success of the refugee rehabilitation ventures in Ahmednagar notwithstanding, there was tangible resentment among the Hindu Mahasabha members against Madanlal and other Sindhi refugees.

Later that day, all six conspirators—Karkare, Badge, Apte, the Godses and Madanlal—took a taxi to the Mota Mandir in Bhuleshwar to secure the ammunition. At the temple, they entered the private chambers of the priest, Goswami Dixitji Maharaj, a well-built forty-five-year-old man of Gujarati descent. He had a long, bearded face and piercing eyes. On the floor of his room lay a khaki drill bag containing five hand grenades, two slabs of explosive material fitted with a detonator and fuse, and a packet of revolver bullets. The bag was packed securely into Madanlal's bedding, which he had carried along. All that was needed for the assassination of Mahatma Gandhi was now ready.

The Final Journey

The six-member squad then parted ways. The Godse brothers, Apte and Badge left for Poona, and Karkare and his protégé Madanlal headed to Bombay's Victoria Terminus station. Before that, Karkare gave Madanlal four rupees and instructions to fetch his clothes from the Dadar Mahasabha office, while he kept the bedding (with the ammunitions bag in it) with himself. Madanlal reached the station at 8 p.m. and occupied a seat in the third-class compartment of the Peshawar Express to Delhi. Half an hour later, Karkare joined him. The bedding containing the bag of ammunition was placed on the upper berth.

Their final journey began.

On 17 January 1948, at noon, their train pulled into the New Delhi railway station. A Marathi-speaking Sindhi was waiting to receive them. They took a tonga to the Birla Mandir near Gole Market, but there were no rooms available. They found a room at the Sharif Hindu Hotel in Fatehpuri—Room No. 2—with a full fare of seven rupees. The hotel had just opened in November 1947. Ramlal Dutt, the fifty-five-year-old manager of the hotel, had previously been a manager at a cotton factory in Pakistan. He had arrived in Delhi in September 1947 and taken over the Sharif Hotel, which used to be a Muslim-run establishment.

Karkare gave his name as B.M. Bias and was referred to as 'Babuji' or 'Lalaji'. He and Madanlal did not know when they would return from their mission, so they gave their clothes for laundry to the one of the hotel-bearers, Ram Singh. At 5 p.m., Karkare left the hotel.

Madanlal was somewhat familiar with Delhi. He had visited Delhi for the first time in 1944. The second time, he was a hapless refugee fleeing west Punjab for Gwalior, with a halt at Delhi. With Karkare away, Madanlal went to meet his maternal uncle, Dr Bal Mukund, in Old Delhi's Chandni Chowk, returning only at 9 p.m. Karkare had still not come back.

When Madanlal awoke the next day, Karkare was already leaving the hotel. He did not think of taking the lowly refugee into confidence. That day Madanlal went to the subzi mandi area in Old Delhi, where Prime Minister Jawaharlal Nehru was to address the crowd. He interrupted Nehru's speech by chanting anti-Pakistan slogans. The police detained him for some time.

The next day, Karkare was in a tearing hurry. He summoned Ram Singh for the laundered clothes and vacated the hotel. Karkare and Madanlal took a tonga to the Hindu Mahasabha office and checked into Room No. 3. It was a sparsely furnished room. Narayan Apte walked in with Shyam Deshpande, the secretary of the Delhi Hindu Mahasabha. Deshpande brought two students with him, who accompanied Madanlal as he went to look for angry refugees in Paharganj, where Hindu refugees had occupied mosques and could cause a disturbance at Mahatma Gandhi's prayer meeting. On their way to Paharganj, they met Om Baba, a mendicant who had been arrested the previous day for fomenting trouble at a prayer meeting.

However, it was nighttime when Madanlal, Karkare, Deshpande and the students reached the Paharganj area. Recruiting at this hour was not possible; most refugees were asleep. Karkare urged the group to leave quickly, as he did not want to be mistaken for a police party who had come to evict the refugees. On their way back, Karkare and Deshpande were in deep conversation. Once again, Madanlal, the dependable foot soldier, felt a little left out, and wished that he could understand Marathi. Back at the Mahasabha, Badge and Kistayya joined in the discussion too. The only thing Madanlal could make out was that they were talking about revolvers. It was almost certain now, if everything went according to plan, that '100 years of Gandhi was going to be over tomorrow.'[15]

The First Attempt

20 January 1948. 6 a.m.

Karkare was already out. Two hours later, Apte and Gopal Godse reached the Hindu Mahasabha office near Birla Mandir. Four members of the squad—Apte, Gopal, Badge and Shankar— went to the deserted ridge behind the office. Shankar returned a short while later, asking for knives and oil.

For two hours, Gopal practised shooting at a tree with a revolver. The squad realized that the revolver was way off the mark. Badge tried to fix it. They spent another half hour practising before returning to the office. Then they headed to the Marina Hotel, where they had taken a room—Room No. 40. However, Madanlal stayed back to wait for Karkare.

At noon, Karkare returned and the duo went to Marina Hotel, armed with the khaki drill bag containing ammunition. In Room No. 40, Apte laid out the plan.

Madanlal was to set off a slab and throw a hand grenade while Shankar had to set off another slab and throw another grenade simultaneously at a different place to create a distraction. Gopal Godse and Badge had to take aim and shoot Gandhi, and then throw a few more hand grenades. Karkare and Nathuram Godse had no direct role; they just had to make sure the plan would be carried out like clockwork.

On 20 January, at around 4 p.m., Madanlal, Digambar Badge, Vishnu Karkare, Narayan Apte and Nathuram and Gopal Godse arrived at Birla House and put their plan to assassinate Mahatma Gandhi into action. A week earlier, on 13 January, Mahatma Gandhi had announced his last satyagraha. Upset that the Indian government had withheld the payment of 55 crore rupees to Pakistan, Gandhi had said that he would only end the fast the day 'peace is restored to Delhi' and a 'Muslim man [can] walk around in the city all by himself'.[16] Madanlal later said,

Mahatma Gandhi's coercion of the Government of India into giving fifty-five crores of rupees to Pakistan drove the iron into my soul. It seems that the faintest whisperings of Delhi Muslims were audible to him but the heaven-rending cry of the Hindu refugees would not penetrate through the solid array of Maulanas and Maulvis Hajis and Hafijies that blocked the way to Mahatmaji's ears. To make this cry of the refugees reach the ears of the Father of the Nation and the Dictator of the Government of India was my sole motive in doing what I did on 20th January 1948.[17] [sic]

The guncotton slab that was ignited looked like a brick, about 9 inches in length, 4 inches in breadth and 2 inches in height. It was white in colour. S.C. Roy, an inspector of explosives from Agra, later analysed the contents of the bomb—it was composed of Baratol and Barium Nitrate, i.e., TNT.

As the bomb exploded, people saw dark green smoke. Women and children were shaking. Madanlal was immediately apprehended by Bhoor Singh, the chowkidar of Birla House.

4

The Beretta Gun that Killed Gandhi

30 January 1948. 5.30 p.m.

THE 'light' had gone out of the lives of Indians. Mahatma Gandhi had succumbed to an assassin's bullets at Birla House (now Gandhi Smriti) in Delhi.

Hit by three bullets in the chest and abdomen, the seventy-eight-year-old fakir collapsed and fell to the ground a few feet away from the pergola where he held daily prayer meetings. His 'walking sticks' and grandnieces, Manu and Abha, also fell down because of the impact. The crowd at Birla House was stunned into silence for a moment. To some, the shots sounded like firecrackers, or a bomb going off, just like it had ten days ago.

Nandlal Mehta, a forty-three-year-old businessman, recounted in his eyewitness account that Abha was on Gandhi's right, Manu on the left and he was right behind them. He was momentarily stunned when the shots went off. When he snapped back, Mahatma Gandhi had collapsed, with spots of blood on his dhoti.

Four constables were on duty that day at Birla House. Amar Nath, the head constable, saw Mahatma Gandhi leave his room at 5.15 p.m., making his way to the prayer ground. The head constable cut across the lawn to walk with Gandhi's entourage. When the gun was fired, he saw smoke. Amar Nath rushed and caught the assailant who had fired the shots. By then the crowd too descended on the killer and Amar Nath received an injury to the head. Sergeant Devraj Singh apprehended the pistol and marched the murderer to the Tughlaq Road police station.

At 6 p.m., All India Radio broadcast the news that Gandhi was no more. As the story began to travel, India went into mourning. In Delhi that night, people flocked to Birla House to catch a glimpse of the Mahatma. Riots broke out in Bombay. Elsewhere, people shut their shops, offices and dispensaries, huddled around radios and congregated on streets. They grieved over this monumental loss, speculated on the identity of the murderer and his motivations, and feared a breakout of communal violence all over again.

A few hundred kilometres away in Gwalior, at 6.30 p.m., life insurance agent Gangadhar Patwardhan heard the news at a wachanalaya (library). Furious discussions ensued over the identity of the killer. Numerous theories were mooted, of which the one that caught on was that this heinous crime was the handiwork of a disgruntled refugee. This particular rumour found legs because Gandhi was repeatedly assailed by angry Hindu and Sikh refugees for his 'appeasement of Muslims'. On 14 January, the second day of his final satyagraha, an irate mob had gathered outside Birla House raising 'Let Gandhi die' slogans. On 20 January, Madanlal Pahwa, a Punjabi refugee, had thrown a guncotton slab in a failed attempt to take Gandhi's life.

When an emotional Jawaharlal Nehru consoled a stunned nation that night in a historic speech, he called the murderer a 'madman' and nothing more. Not too many details were public yet; the identity of the murderer was still unknown. In fact, DSP Jaswant Singh was yet to record Nathuram Godse's statement.

At around 9 p.m., Gangadhar Patwardhan went home, which was located behind the Rajput Boarding House in the city of Lashkar—one of the three regions of the Greater Gwalior state. His first-floor neighbour, Madhukar Balkrishna Khire, was already home. They talked about Mahatma Gandhi's assassination in utter disbelief and shock. However, when Patwardhan told him about the theory that murderer might have been a refugee, Khire corrected him. 'It was a Maharashtrian,' he told his bewildered friend. A little while later that night, Khire left for Delhi on the Peshawar Express, presumably to poke around for more details on the assassination.

Khire was a twenty-year-old student who had lived in Gwalior for ten years. He was a staunch believer in the Hindu Mahasabha. He was also a member of the militant Hindu outfit in Gwalior, the Hindu Rashtra Sena, founded by Dattatreya Parchure, a well-known Ayurvedic doctor in the city.

On 30 January, Khire heard the news of Gandhi's assassination at around 6 p.m. He went straight to Parchure's house, situated on the main road of Gwalior. According to some, Parchure was a figure of importance in Gwalior; his dispensary was a hub of political activity. In fact, this Hindu leader had been at the forefront of staging vociferous protests against the interim government that was put in place after Independence, even offering to go on satyagraha. Khire met Parchure and asked him to call off his protests because of the murder. When he asked the doctor who could have committed this act, Parchure said, 'Someone like us.'

Both Khire and Parchure walked to the Rajput Boarding House, where the doctor exchanged a few words with the proprietor, Ram Dayal Singh. When they returned to the house, the radio was on and some sweets were being served as if it was a celebratory occasion. Khire took some sweets and told Parchure that he was going to Delhi for Gandhi's funeral. On 31 January, Khire was among the thousands of people who had gathered in Delhi to have one final darshan of Mahatma Gandhi.[1]

31 January 1948

The world now knew who had killed Gandhi. The name of Nathuram Godse was first broadcast by the British Broadcasting Service (BBC) and then by AIR. Patwardhan grew increasingly anxious; how did Khire know that the murderer was a Maharashtrian? When Khire returned to Gwalior on 1 February, Patwardhan went to confront him. After a lot of persuasion, Khire reluctantly revealed his source: Parchure.

Patwardhan was seriously alarmed. It seemed to him that he was embroiled with the group that might have been responsible for Mahatma Gandhi's assassination. Patwardhan also came to know that the group had been aware of Nathuram Godse's presence in Gwalior. He grew paranoid. On 2 February, he went to meet his friend Madhukar Keshav Kale, who was an employee of Gwalior state. Patwardhan wanted to tell all to his friend—the conversations with Khire, the revelations and the suspicions. But he was in for a rude shock. It appeared that his friend knew even more about the murder than his neighbour.

The eldest of four sons, Kale was a graduate and a member of the militant HRS since 1940–41, which he had joined on the insistence of Nilkantha aka Nilu, his friend and Parchure's son. He had left the HRS in May 1947 when he took up a job with the Gwalior state. His family had disapproved of his association with the militant organization; in fact, his mother Rukmini Bai even asked Parchure to stop 'misleading' her son. Before Kale severed ties, he'd enjoyed the physical training offered by the organization. At HRS, Kale learned to wield lathis, swish swords and throw spears. Physical training was a key feature of Hindutva organizations. The objective was that Hindutvawadis should be able to stop outsiders (read Muslims) from taking over their motherland with their sheer physical might. The HRS called upon all able-bodied Hindu men to build their physique and stamina by way of drills, to prepare for a fight against an imaginary Muslim onslaught.[2]

Even though Kale had stopped going to the HRS, he continued to visit Parchure and his family. Politics was often a topic of heated conversation, especially Gandhi, the Congress and their pro-Muslim bent. It was not unusual for Kale to hear Parchure hold Gandhi responsible for the Congress's Muslim appeasement policies; the doctor-commander often said, 'As the flow of water must be stopped at its origin, like that Congress will not change its Muslim-appeasing policy until Mahatma Gandhi has been finished.'[3]

On that fateful evening of 30 January, Kale heard of Gandhi's death on the radio. He then met Parchure outside the Maratha Boarding House before Madhukar Khire met him at the dispensary a little while later. Parchure was strolling with another man—a turban-wearing Maratha. Kale informed Parchure of this historic development. At first Parchure wanted to be sure—had Gandhi died or was he murdered? Kale pressed on, saying that this was the day the 'water had ceased to flow', like Parchure had said. But the doctor simply shrugged it off, refusing to make any more of the murder. 'One great demon of the world is dead and no time will be required to form a Hindu Samrajya,' he said. It was almost as if he had expected this.

In fact, Parchure had dropped many hints about the assassination to different people in Gwalior, so much so that his remarks became the key to unravel the conspiracy behind Mahatma Gandhi's murder.

Ram Dayal Singh, owner of the Rajput Boarding House and president of the Rajput Seva Sangh, said in his witness statement that Parchure had come to his boarding house on 30 January and blurted out that 'a good deed has been done'. He had further added that the opponent of Hindu religion had been killed and now Hinduism would be safe. It has also been recorded that Parchure sometimes referred to Gandhi as an 'avatar of Aurangazeb'.

Ram Dayal Singh said that Parchure had a habit of claiming credit for things that were happening. '*Gandhiji ko marne wala apna aadmi tha* (The man who killed Gandhi is one of ours),' Parchure is reported to have said. His talk only got bigger; Parchure claimed that the bomb explosion of 20 January was also the work of their man and that the pistol used to kill Gandhi was from Gwalior.

On the morning of 30 January, another witness, Jagannath Singh, had gone to the Rajput Boarding House to discuss the future of Rajputs in the interim government's ministry. He had proposed that the HRS join in their demand, to which Parchure replied that something was going to be completed in a day or two.

On 31 January, Kale, along with the rest of the world, found out that Nathuram Vinayak Godse was the name of Gandhi's murderer. Kale was familiar with the name, because Parchure's son Nilkantha had told him on 28 January that Godse had paid them a visit. Kale had passed on this information to his mother and some friends. On 2 February, when Patwardhan went to visit Kale, his neighbourhood of Lashkar was already buzzing with the rumour that Godse had come to Gwalior some days back to pay a visit to Parchure. Patwardhan grew anxious and threatened Kale. He went to Kale's house several times that day.

On one occasion Madhukar Khire accompanied him and heard Kale's story.

According to Kale, Patwardhan was not just an insurance agent but also a police informer. Armed with this explosive information about Godse's presence in Gwalior, Patwardhan forced Kale to go to the government. He was taking steps to distance himself from this group that was multiplying like a hydra.

Later that day, the police informer, the state service employee and the student went to seek an audience with Gwalior state's home minister, Murlidhar Ghule, in Patwardhan's Studebaker. They were received because of the urgency of the matter and its connection to Gandhi's assassination.

It so happened that Muralidhar Ghule and Dattatreya Parchure had a history of bad blood. On the day of the Indian independence, the Maharaja of Gwalior, Jivajirao Scindia, had announced the reconstitution of his cabinet to include five non-officials—three Congress members, one Dalit member and one Muslim member—and decided 22 January 1948 as the date for the inauguration of the newly constituted government. The reconstituted cabinet, which had excluded the Hindu Mahasabha altogether, came as a shock to Parchure. He was so livid that he wrote to the dewan of Gwalior state, M.A. Sreenivasan, for a meeting. In his memoirs, Sreenivasan later recalled that meeting with an irate Parchure. The doctor came to the meeting with Narayan Apte. They were offered tea, which they drank in silence. Sreenivasan wrote that the saucer trembled and rattled in Parchure's hands, he was that angry. 'Why have you excluded us from the cabinet? You have betrayed us. You are a betrayer of Hinduism, you and your Gandhi,' Parchure told him. Still angry, he mockingly recited a distortion of Gandhi's favourite bhajan, '*Raghupati Raghava Ram Rahim, pateeta pavana Krishna Karim!*'[4]

Gandhi's prayer meetings in September 1947, held every day in the evening at the Birla House, included recitations from the Bhagavad Gita and the Quran. At the time Delhi was in the grip of communal violence. There were also times when Gandhi's prayer meetings were disturbed by Hindu refugees who objected to the recital of the Quran. K.N. Sahaney, a lawyer who came to Delhi from Rawalpindi in 1947, said he had seen one or two such disturbances in his witness statement. But he also said that he had never heard Parchure's version of the bhajan sung at the prayer meetings.

The doctor continued to threaten the government official. 'We shall finish you both. We have hand grenades,' he said, at which point the dewan ended the conversation and escorted them out.

Sreenivasan gave a report of this conversation to the Maharaja. He also wrote that the speeches of the Mahasabha and RSS leaders in the state were abusive and the crowds were getting unruly.

In late August 1947, Parchure and the Hindu Mahasabha branch in Gwalior started an agitation for political reforms in the princely state. The doctor was subsequently arrested. Madanlal was also present at the agitation. It was only two months later, in October, that Parchure and other Hindu Mahasabhites were released by the state. Between 24 and 28 January 1948, the Hindu Mahasabha staged a demonstration against the newly constituted Congress-led government in Gwalior state.

As he heard Patwardhan out, Ghule understood the enormous significance of Parchure's role in Mahatma Gandhi's assassination.

At around the same time in Delhi, DSP Sardar Jaswant Singh and his team was confronting Godse, asking him to explain the Gwalior ticket he had used to secure the waiting room at New Delhi Railway Station. In his interrogation, Godse denied visiting Gwalior. He claimed that it was a fake ticket, issued by the keeper of the waiting room, who took a bribe of five rupees to allow him access to it.

Despite Godse's unruffled denials, it was only a matter of a couple of hours before Jaswant Singh got his breakthrough from Gwalior.

3 February 1948

The special superintendent of police (SSP), Railways, United Province, was travelling from Mathura Cantonment to Jhansi. At Gwalior, the station officer (Government railway police) tipped him off that on the day of Mahatma Gandhi's assassination, a Hindu Mahasabha leader had distributed sweets to members of his party and had asked them to tune into the news on radio that evening without fail. On 30 January 1948, after Mahatma Gandhi was shot, Parchure had sent his domestic help Rupa Mehrat to the market in Gwalior to purchase sweets for four rupees and distribute them among his friends and family.

News has a habit of travelling fast.

Muralidhar Ghule again lost no time. He ordered the Superintendent of Police (SP) Thorat Patil to arrest Dattatreya Parchure. On 3 February Parchure was detained, like many others with links to Hindu right-wing organizations across north India. Handed over to the military police, Parchure was taken to the Gwalior Fort. In the meantime, the Gwalior police dispatched CID Inspector Shankar Rao to Delhi with the information pertaining to the Gwalior link to Bapu's murder.

Rao returned from Delhi three days later, on 6 February. In a strange coincidence, he hailed a Muslim tongawala called Jumma. They got to talking and soon, Rao knew the sequence of events from the time Nathuram Godse and Narayan Apte had arrived in Gwalior.

27 January 1948

At around 11.30 p.m., two passengers alighted from the Peshawar Express at the Gwalior railway station. The train came from Bombay, not Peshawar as it used to before Partition. One of the passengers wore white pants; the other was clad in a dhoti. It was still quite chilly, so the trouser-clad man covered his head with a muffler while the dhoti-wearer was wrapped up in a blanket. Outside the station, a tongawala named Ghariba persuaded them to get on his vehicle. The fare was fixed at one rupee. The tonga had only reached the second-class platform when the horse became unruly and broke out of the harness. Ghariba's passengers got off.

Another tongawala, Jumma, was waiting next to the second-class waiting room, near the station's cycle stand, for customers. Ghariba asked his fellow tongawala to help his passengers out. The two men climbed on to Jumma's tonga, carrying one bag and a bedding. Their destination: Nadi Gate Bridge in Shinde ki Chhavni, to Parchure's house.

There was no difficulty in the locating the address. The self-styled dictator of the HRS was a leading Hindu Mahasabhite and a vocal, militant Hindu voice in Gwalior. Just a few days ago, Parchure had organized a rally with nearly 900 RSS volunteers in Gwalior to protest the non-inclusion of the Hindu Mahasabha in the newly formed government, much like the agitation he had started against the Gwalior princely state in 1947.

As they neared Parchure's house, one of the passengers asked Jumma to inquire about the exact location. The visitors did this as a precaution; they were simply confirming that Jumma, a Muslim, was not trying to get them killed in a Muslim 'ghetto'. In reality, the opposite was true. Jumma said that there had been several communal disturbances in Gwalior in 1947, during which many Muslims shifted out of the city. Fearing the Hindu Mahasabha, Jumma himself had moved base to Lashkar city.

An elderly washerwoman gave them directions to the doctor's residence—the red house near an electric pole. It was almost midnight. The man in trousers got down from the tonga and knocked on the door. Nilkantha was awake, studying in his room. He opened the window to find out who had knocked on their door at this hour. The visitors told him that they were there to meet with his father and gave him their names. Nilu went upstairs to wake up his father. Together, they opened the door. One of the men stepped inside and announced, 'I, Nathuram Godse, have come.'

Godse was the one dressed in white pants, a warm coat and muffler. The man wearing the dhoti, along with a chocolate-brown checked coat and woollen cap, was none other than Narayan Apte. This was not the first time Godse had visited Parchure; around five years ago, the doctor's family had looked after him when he had fallen sick while travelling through Gwalior.

That night, Parchure had retired to his room by 10.45 p.m. At midnight, Nilu woke him up, informing him of the two visitors—Godse and Apte. Parchure knew these names well.

Born in Poona, Parchure had completed his preliminary education before moving to and settling in Gwalior at the turn of the twentieth century. He came from a privileged Brahmin household; his father had served as education minister in Gwalior and his elder brother was secretary to the Gwalior government in 1947. Parchure had completed his medical studies from the legendary Grant Medical College, Bombay, in 1931, and joined the Gwalior state medical service before he was dismissed in 1934 for forging a medical certificate. Thereafter, he opened his dispensary in Lashkar colony, home also to Gangadhar Patwardhan.

In 1939, two years after Vinayak Savarkar became the Hindu Mahasabha president, Parchure opened its branch in Gwalior state. In 1940, he founded his own organization, the HRS. Over a period of eight years, it recruited nearly 2,000 volunteers. In the first week of August 1942, Parchure travelled to Bombay and Poona. Until then, he had never met Savarkar. In Poona, he met Nathuram Godse. He tried to make a case for their organizations to work together.

In 1944, Parchure went again to Bombay and Poona. In his own words, 'I, being a rashtrawadi [nationalist], was coming in closer contact with V.D. Savarkar.'[5] That year, Parchure became the president of the Gwalior chapter of the Hindu Mahasabha.

On 8 August 1947, Parchure met with Godse, Apte and Savarkar in Delhi at the All India Hindu Mahasabha working committee meeting. This was the first time that all the accused in the conspiracy to murder Gandhi met up.

*

Although Parchure knew Godse and Apte, he wasn't expecting them in Gwalior. When they told him they were there on a special mission, the doctor sent his son out of the room to prepare tea for the guests. Once he was sure they were alone, he repeated his question—why had they come to Gwalior?

'We have decided to finish Gandhi before 2 February, because after the second, Gandhi is going out of Delhi,' was the reply.[6] Then Godse pulled the revolver meant for assassinating Gandhi out of his coat. It wasn't a good gun, he said. They had come to Gwalior to seek Parchure's help in getting a good revolver that would get the job done. When the duo told him about Madanlal's failed attempt, Parchure realized that it was also part of their conspiracy and the mission was serious.

Parchure examined the weapon; it was a small, country-made gun. Then he gave his assurance to the visitors: he would help them acquire a better gun.

The tea arrived. Godse declined but Apte had a cup. The hall was cleared for them to sleep. They did not have a lot of luggage—a khaki bedding and a khaki-coloured handbag. At around 12.30, everyone retired for the night.

In the morning, Parchure sent Nilu and his domestic worker Rupa Mehrat to fetch Gangadhar Dandwate, his close confidant. It would do well to remember that the state of Gwalior had not escaped the communal frenzy that followed the Partition. In fact, Parchure's militant outfit was at the forefront of stoking communal tension. Gangadhar Dandwate was their arms supplier.

At around noon, Dandwate arrived at the red house near the electric pole. He brought a revolver with him. The four of them—Parchure, Dandwate, Godse and Apte—went to the courtyard to test the gun. Unsatisfied with it, the visitors asked for a better one. Dandwate promised to arrange one by that evening.

8 February 1948

DSP Sardar Jaswant Singh was interrogating Nathuram Godse with the new detailed information received on the Gwalior connection. Godse denied it all. His testimony remained unchanged: he and Narayan Apte went to New Delhi Railway Station immediately after the assassination attempt on 20 January. He bought two first-class tickets to Cawnpore (now

Kanpur) on a Bombay-bound train that departed from Delhi between 9 and 10 p.m. that night. They arrived in Cawnpore, where they killed time in a retiring room. On 27 January, they were back at the New Delhi Railway Station, trying to reserve space in the retiring room until 29 January, which Godse managed at last by paying a bribe of five rupees in addition to the waiting fare to the booking clerk, Sundar Lal. Mrs Angelina Coleston, the matron at Kanpur Central Railway Station, saw Godse and Apte in the first class retiring room on 22 January at the same time when the Lucknow-Jhansi mail arrived. They were shabbily dressed, according to her, and were carrying a small attaché and bedding.[7]

Godse's testimony was only partly true. Jaswant Singh had already begun to piece together the Gwalior connection to the assassination.

28 January, 12 p.m.

Madhukar Kale took leave from office. He went to Baldeo Bank to withdraw thirty rupees. Then, as per his usual routine, he dropped by at Parchure's house. The doctor was sitting on an easy chair in the hall. Kale wanted to find out what the Hindu Mahasabha intended to do now that the interim government had been handed over to the Congress. He crossed the veranda to reach the hall, where a few guests were present. Two of them were trying out a revolver and filling the gun with cartridges, while a third guest looked on. The taller one of the two was successful in pulling the trigger, while the other was not. They continued to practise, loading the barrel one cartridge at a time. They told the third guest, Gangadhar Dandwate, that they needed better revolvers. If not revolvers, then good pistols. Dandwate took the gun from their hands and fired off a few rounds. The revolver was good, he said to the two guests. One of them tried to fire it once again but he could not pull the trigger. This was a country-made revolver. The two men repeated their request for a good pistol as they wanted to leave Gwalior that afternoon. Dandwate asked Parchure to loan his own gun, but the doctor refused. Dandwate took back the revolver, put it in his pocket and promised the two men a better-quality pistol before evening. He suggested that they catch the night train from Gwalior. He took five currency notes from them and left. The rest of them ate lunch and then Kale went back to the bank. Later in the evening, he ran into Dandwate near Falka Bazaar. He asked Dandwate if he had managed to arrange a pistol.

'Yes,' said Dandwate.

At Parchure's house, the doctor retired for a siesta after the meal. Godse and Apte too napped in the hall. Later that afternoon, a fourth guest arrived at Parchure's—Jagdish Prasad Goel. Twenty-four-year-old Goel was the principal officer of Parchure's HRS. Goel had previously met Narayan Apte and Savarkar's secretary Damle. He was meeting Apte again on 28 January. He also knew Godse, having met him at Parchure's two years ago. Goel knew everybody there through his Hindu Mahasabha links. In fact, besides Godse and Apte, he even knew Savarkar's secretary Damle. They talked of Gwalior politics, after which Goel took their leave.

At 5 p.m., Nilu stepped out of the house just as Dandwate arrived on his cycle. He was finding it difficult to arrange for a good revolver at such short notice. He wanted to talk to Parchure, Godse and Apte about securing Jagdish Goel's pistol. Parchure agreed with his plan. Later that night, Dandwate asked Goel for his pistol. The latter agreed on one condition—that either his pistol be replaced or he be given 500 rupees. At 8.30 p.m., Dandwate returned to Parchure's house, where all four of them huddled in the doctor's room. They remained there for the next two and a half hours. Dandwate showed them a pistol—an Italian-made automatic pistol No. 719791, Beretta CAL 9, manufactured in 1934. Godse and Apte took turns to check the pistol, take out its magazine and fill it with seven cartridges. Then they tried the safety catch. It was good to go.

Apte paid Dandwate 300 rupees. He would send the balance later, he said. Then Apte went out for dinner while Godse skipped the meal altogether. At 10.30 p.m., Godse and Apte packed their bedding and bag. Dandwate hailed a tonga passing by; Godse and Apte went off on their way. Two things were certain—there was a gun and a gunner to kill Mahatma Gandhi.

The next day, 29 January, Madhukar Kale ran into Nilu. Kale was curious about Parchure's guests. Nilu did not see any reason to conceal their names. 'Godse and Apte,' he told Kale.

Kale had heard of Godse as the editor of the publication *Dainik Agrani*, so he asked again: 'Nathuram Godse?'

'Yes,' Nilu confirmed.

*

After the failed attempt to kill Gandhi on 20 January 1948, the assassination squad knew that the police were on their trail. Most of the seven members had dispersed in panic; Madanlal was immediately arrested, and only Godse and Apte remained together. The duo was confident of making another attempt before Mahatma Gandhi left Delhi on 2 February 1948.

On 23 January, they reached Bombay at 8 p.m. via the Punjab Mail that arrived from Cawnpore. They could not secure a room, so they spent the night in the second-class waiting room. This was their second night in a row in railway-station waiting rooms. They checked into the Elphinstone Hotel the next day under the aliases N. Vinayak Rao and B. Narain Rao. They discussed plans. Apte was reluctant to go with a plan that had no option to escape. But Godse thought otherwise. He believed that an individual sacrifice was necessary to carry out this plan. He felt that this act would be essential to their revolutionary cause, so he volunteered. His partner in the ultimate crime, Apte, did not want him to go alone, so he kept looking for alternatives. However, there was little time to lose. Godse was unwilling to risk more than two days for an alternate plan to emerge.

On 29 January, they arrived at the New Delhi Railway Station and tried to secure the retiring room. After some negotiation, Godse paid ten rupees—one half of it as room fare and the other half as a bribe—to the booking clerk, Sundar Lal. Apte was still looking for alternatives, but coming up short.

30 January 1948, 3 p.m.

Nathuram Godse and Narayan Apte parted ways. Godse took a tonga to the Birla Mandir and spent some time in front of the statues of Shivaji and Baji Rao Peshwa. Then he took another tonga, this time to Birla House. A fully loaded Beretta with seven bullets lay hidden in one of his trouser pockets. He went inside and took his place in the crowd that had lined up to greet Gandhi.

At 5.17 p.m., the crowd spotted Mahatma Gandhi. As the fragile old fakir walked down the path towards him, Godse slipped his hand inside his pocket.

Book II
The Monarch

1

An Open Secret

26 January 1948

FOUR days before Gandhi's assassination, DSP Kartar Singh generated a secret note based on the interrogation of Madanlal Pahwa.

The note was organized into two parts: 'Engaged in the conspiracy' and 'Names mentioned in the statement'.

In the first part, 'Engaged in the conspiracy', Madanlal could not give the names of the seven people who were involved, except for his primary contact, Vishnu Karkare. But he did give vivid descriptions of everyone else whose identities were later established as the key conspirators in the case.

The second part, 'Names mentioned in the statement', was of more interest. The ninth name was 'Veer Savarkar'.[1]

It was not the first time that Madanlal had mentioned Savarkar's name in connection with Gandhi's assassination.

There was a second, independent confirmation of Madanlal's story about Savarkar and the conspiracy to kill Gandhi. More than a fortnight before this secret note was generated, on 10 January 1948, Madanlal had gone to meet Professor J.C. Jain, who had helped him during his early days as a refugee in Bombay, with Karkare. After Karkare left Professor Jain's house, Madanlal, who stayed on, told the latter that 'Kirkree [Karkare] financing a party which they had formed and it was collecting arms and ammunitions [sic]'. While narrating his exploits to the professor, Madanlal told him that Savarkar had 'sent for him and talked for a considerable time, after which Savarkar patted him on the back and said, "Carry on"'.[2]

Madanlal informed Professor Jain that 'he also told Savarkar that he had been entrusted with the work of throwing bomb in the prayer-ground of Mahatma Ji and to create confusion and that Mahatma Ji will be over-powered by the members of his party [sic]'.[3]

Jain did not take Madanlal seriously until he read about the failed assassination attempt on 20 January 1948. After that the professor immediately met with Morarji Desai, the then home minister of Bombay Presidency, and informed him about Madanlal and Karkare's visit and the details the former had told him about the assassination plot.

Desai met with Bombay Police's Deputy Commissioner J.D. Nagarwala, who was handling the intelligence portfolio, the same night at 8.15 p.m. at the railway station, as Nagarwala was about to depart for Ahmedabad. His instructions to the deputy commissioner were clear—arrest Karkare and keep a close watch on Savarkar's house. The court which tried the Gandhi assassination case, as well as the Kapur Commission, that was set up to re-examine it, also confirmed that Morarji Desai did convey the information Jain gave him to Nagarwala.

On the morning of 22 January 1948, Desai met with Union Home Minister Sardar Vallabhbhai Patel and narrated the whole incident to him.

The reason why the police failed to nab the assassins well in time was attributed to them not having the conspirators' exact names, although there were ample leads, such as Madanlal identifying Nathuram Godse as the editor of the *Dainik Agrani*, the old name of his right-wing publication, *Hindu Rashtra*.

It is intriguing why the other conspirators did not give Madanlal their real names. After all, Madanlal had been recruited for a very sensitive and secretive mission. There can be many reasons. While there were people willing to kill and be killed for the cause of refugee Hindus from Pakistan, an oft-heard story was that the refugees were not fully accepted in India at the time. Was it that the others feared that Madanlal would leak their names? Or was he meant to be the scapegoat in the plan if it went horribly wrong?

Madanlal was also the only outsider in the squad. Nathuram Godse and Narayan Apte had been professionally associated. Gopal Godse was Nathuram's brother. Vishnu Karkare was an associate of Apte. Karkare knew Digambar Badge and Shankar Kistayya was Badge's servant.

The failure to stop Gandhi's assassination despite prior 'actionable' information remains perhaps the biggest intelligence lapse in the history of India.

No Broken Promises

As mentioned in an earlier chapter, post Mahatma Gandhi's assassination DSP Jaswant Singh interrogated Godse for three consecutive days to confirm Savarkar's role. However, Godse did not crack, except for revealing that he came to Delhi with Apte. Singh quizzed Godse for the first time on the afternoon of 1 February 1948 jointly with Kartar Singh and Mehta Bal Krishna, an inspector in the CID office. On 2 February, the interrogation started at 10 a.m. and continued till 7 p.m. On the third day, the interrogation started at around 1 p.m. So far, Godse was sticking to his version that he had masterminded the assassination. Jaswant Singh noted , as mentioned earlier, with frustration, 'I continued interrogating Godse accused at Parliamentary street police Station, but nothing useful was revealed.'[4]

Remember, Godse went to Birla House prepared to kill Gandhi and be killed either by the crowd or the state. Nothing could reduce his determination to assassinate a man who, in his mind, was anti-national. But it is a little surprising that he was trying to save his friends and co-conspirators by pleading guilty. Perhaps all the actors did not anticipate so much information to come on record.

While the police and the nation were still gasping at the assassination of Gandhi, the Hindu Mahasabha was sheltering the conspirators. On 31 January 1948 at 7.22 p.m., V.G. Deshpande, secretary, Hindu Mahasabha Bhawan, received a telegram: 'Arriving Delhi arrange for defence.'[5]

The messenger was Apte. DSP Singh was passed on this intel by the Bombay police and it was verified by the Calcutta police from the Central Telegraph Office. The Hindu Mahasabha was emerging as the epicentre of this assassination.

Post Gandhi's assassination, the intelligence network started picking up leads. One such report dated 2 March 1948 gave a useful tip to the probe team about Ram Singh, a servant at the Hindu Mahasabha Bhawan who was said to be a trusted aide of Ashutosh Lahiri, the All India secretary of the Hindu Mahasabha. Ram Singh was interrogated and helped the police identify the accused. Lahiri was one of the first to be arrested for the murder. Ram Singh had been living with Madanlal in the same room in Hindu Mahasabha Bhawan. The intelligence was quite specific: 'Kirkree is believed to have sent a message or a letter to Ashutosh Lahiri from Cawnpore to arrange for Madan Lal's defence [sic]. The letter in question is said to have since been destroyed.'[6]

On 26 January 1948, Lahiri was in Bombay to meet Savarkar. They met again the next day at 10.30 a.m. Lahiri claimed that their meeting was strictly about two topics related to the Hindu Mahasabha: the reorientation policy of the sabha and the appointment of an acting president in case Savarkar was elected as the president.

It was not just Lahiri who had come to meet Savarkar. In the preceding days Apte and Godse had also visited Savarkar after the failed assassination attempt on 20 January.

The case diary of J.D. Nagarwala noted the following findings: 'In the course of interrogation of accused N.V Godse is transpired that on 23.1.48 he had taken food in the colony restaurant at Dadar after meeting Sawarkar.'[7] [sic]
This was corroborated by the owner of the restaurant.

A statement of Sitaram Anantrao Shate, proprietor of the Colony restaurant, Shivaji Park, Dadar was recorded on 26.2.48. He states that most of the visitors to Savarkar have their meals in his hotel and sometimes the money was paid by Damle, V.D Sawarkar's secretary. He says that he knows Apte and Nathuram Godse, and between 23rd and 25th Jan'48 Nathuram had visited his hotel for food and at that time he was found particularly in a confused state of mind.[8] [sic]

As mentioned in the chapter 'The August Conspiracy', an intelligence report from the Gwalior Crime Investigation Department dated 30 January was quoted as saying that Godse was sent to Parchure, who supplied the Beretta gun to kill Gandhi, by Savarkar.

The investigation by the Bombay Police under Nagarwala conclusively provided evidence of Savarkar's involvement in the conspiracy. The fact that Godse and Apte had been in touch with Savarkar before and after the earlier attempt and ahead of the actual assassination was proved beyond doubt.

The case diary of 1 February 1948 contained crucial evidence which never saw the light of the day until the late 1960s, well after Savarkar was dead. It said: 'Minute enquiries were started with Gajanan Vishnu Damle, Appa Ramachandra Kasar, Balraj Mehta, Laxman Ganesh Chatte, and Avtar Singh, Harman Singh Bedi who were brought to the office of interrogation.'[9] [sic]

The diary continued:

During the course of separate interrogation of the first two named persons it was learnt that Nathuram Vinayak Godse, accompanied by Narayan Dattatraya Apte, had seen Sawarkar twice or thrice before the bomb explosion on 20. 1.1948.[sic]

Both the persons denied, however, any personal knowledge. It was also learnt from these persons that about a week or so before the explosion of the 20th Jan Karkare from Ahmednagar who is an active Hindu Mahasabhaite and who had gone to Noakhali to oppose the tour of Gandhiji and to create agitation against Gandhiji's peace mission in Noakhali, had also come to see Sawarkar. [sic]

Karkare was accompanied by a young Punjabi aged about 23/25, whose name they learnt later on to be Madan Lal and who was involved in the bomb explosion of the 20th Jan. Karkare and Madan Lal had about an hour's talk with Sawarkar. Both the persons are not prepared to depose as to what took place at the Sawarkar's meeting. These two persons also stated that one Badge, owner of Maharashtra Shastra Bhandar of Poona, also used to come to see Sawarkar. Apte and Godse had free access to see Sawarkar, without previous appointment or having to wait downstairs, but others had to wait till Sawarkar agreed to see them.[10] [sic]

Savarkar denied any such meetings. He stuck to his stand during the trial. It was based on this 'inconclusive' evidence that the trial court acquitted him. The prosecution never contradicted Savarkar with Damle's and Apparao's statements during the trial. These facts remained undisclosed to the public until the Kapur Commission reports.

But Nagarwala had no doubts in his mind.

'From the story related by these two persons it appears that it was at these meetings of Sawarkar with these two individuals that the plan to do away with Mahatmaji was finalized [sic],' Nagarwala concluded in his case diary of 1 February 1948.[11]

No Surprises

At 2.30 p.m. on 1 February, Nagarwala searched Savarkar's house, Savarkar Sadan, in Dadar. He said that when they reached, it was as if Savarkar knew why the police had come. 'When the police party under me arrived for searching Sawarkar's house, Mr. V.D Savarkar met the party in the front room and asked me whether I had come to arrest him in the connection with Gandhiji's murder.'[12] [sic]

For the followers of Hindutva, Savarkar was as important a figure as Gandhi. Following Gandhi's assassination, the crackdown on the right wing had started and many RSS and prominent Hindutva leaders had been arrested. The police was treading carefully, given that in both Delhi and Bombay their departments already mishandled the case, leading to the death of the Father of the Nation.

Nagarwala told Savarkar that they were at his house to conduct a search in connection with Gandhi's assassination. 'Sawarkar [sic] pretended to be ill and went into the inside room to lie down.'[13]

Nothing substantial that directly linked him to the assassination was recovered from Savarkar's house, except past letters between him and Nathuram Godse.

But the case against him was getting tighter.

By 4 February 1948, the Bombay Police had obtained custody of Madanlal.

Nagarwala recorded on 6 February 1948:

It was confirmed by Madan Lal that he had been taken by V.R. Karkare (absconding accused) to the residence of V.D. Sawarkar at Shivaji Park, Dadar, and was placed before V.D. Sawarkar when he was complemented by him in connection with the work that he was doing and exhorted him to continue his good work. This interview was stated to be on or about 10th Jan. 1948.[14] [sic]

An identification parade was arranged at about 5.30 p.m. on 6 February 1948 in the Arthur Road prison where V.D. Savarkar had been detained. Madanlal and Kistayya were to identify him. Both the accused were kept outside the prison in a closed van till the identification parade was to happen.

'Madan Lal identified V.D.Savarkar as the person known to him in connection with the hand grenade.'[15]

By the end of February, there was no doubt in Nagarwala's mind about whose mishandling of the case after the 20 January assassination attempt resulted in not identifying Godse and Apte as the key conspirators.

He concluded in his case diary of 23 February 1948:

> From the trend of interrogation of accused Apte, Karkare, Nathuram Godse, it appears that the influence of V.D. Savarkar had played a great part on their minds in the political sphere and ultimately resulted in the assassination of mahatmaji. It is also certain that they have committed this offence to satisfy Sawarkar and his revolutionary political ideology and under the direct orders of Sawakar.[16] [sic]

Savarkar was formally arrested on the charges of conspiracy in the assassination of Gandhi.

Nobody Conspired to Kill Gandhi

31 January 1948

A day after the assassination, only Nathuram Godse and Madanlal were in police custody. Godse was adamant that Gandhi needed to be killed in the 'national interest'. He refused to name any others in the conspiracy.

On the same day, Apte went to take legal advice from Jamandas Mehta, who incidentally became Savarkar's counsel. It was on his advice that Apte decided to not to go to Delhi despite sending the telegram mentioned earlier to Lahiri for arranging his defence.

During the trial, Savarkar denied any part in the conspiracy of Gandhi's assassination.

I say there never was any agreement and conspiracy to murder Gandhiji among the accused or any of them and that the suggestion made by the Prosecution to that effect is entirely without foundation ... I say that there was no conspiracy and/or no attempt to murder Gandhiji at any time or period of time or on or about the 20th January 1948, that I was never party to the blowing up of any bomb or gun cotton slab and that what took place on the 30th January 1948 in the evening at Birla House at the time of Gandhiji's prayer meeting was without my knowledge or consent or complicity of any kind.[17] [sic]

On the contrary, a day before the failed assassination attempt, 19 January 1948, a trunk call was booked from Phone No. 8024, which was the phone number of the Hindu Mahasabha Bhawan, New Delhi, to Phone No. 60201 in Bombay. It was booked at 11.15 a.m. The person who booked the call did not give his name but wanted to talk to 'Damle or Kasar'. It was an urgent and personal call, but the people he asked for could not attend the call, so it remained incomplete. P.K. Kaila, who worked in the Telephone Revenue Office that kept a record of all trunk calls from Delhi, confirmed that on 19 January 1948, such a trunk call was booked from Delhi to Bombay.

'According to the source report the man who booked the call from Delhi was Apte accused from H.M.S Bhawan telephone [sic],'[18] as per the case diary of 20 March 1948.

'Damle' was Gajanan Vishnu Damle, Savarkar's secretary, and 'Kasar' was Appa Ramachandra Kasar, Savarkar's bodyguard. Both of them had already given statements to the police that the squad that was behind the failed attempt had visited Savarkar at his house 'twice or thrice'. However, for reasons best known to the prosecution, neither were their statements recorded in court nor were they brought in as witnesses to counter Savarkar's argument.

Madanlal and Kistayya had given similar statements as well. To this Savarkar's response was:

I beg to reassert that whosoever might be the author of the story of Madan Lal's visit to me, it is altogether false. I had never heard of Madan Lal nor had I ever met him. I submit once again that Madan Lal never met me nor had I any conversation with him at any time whatsoever ...[19] [sic]

Savarkar went on distancing himself from each of the accused.

'Dr Parchure used to send me reports of the Hindu Mahasabha work at Gwalior for a few years ... Since my resignation of the Presidentship some four years ago I had heard nothing from Dr Parchure,' he further stated before the court.[20]

Here again, the prosecution did not produce the intelligence report from Gwalior which had said, well in advance of the assassination, that Savarkar had referred Godse to Parchure. The author of the report was not brought in as a witness either.

On 10 November 1948, Apte, in his statement before the court during the cross-examination, vehemently denied going to Gwalior for procuring the gun that killed Gandhi.

> It is an absurdity on the part of the prosecution to suggest that Nathuram Godse and I had gone to Gwalior to procure a pistol. As a matter of fact we were in a position to have procured a revolver or a pistol, if required, at Bombay or Poona. Volunteers for staging a demonstration at Delhi were not forthcoming in sufficient number at Bombay. We were short of funds. We were very keen that a demonstration be staged at Delhi as early as possible as we expected that we might be arrested in connection with the explosion incident that had taken place at the Birla House on 20th January 1948. We had read in the newspapers that the Police had already raided the Mariana Hotel. We accordingly decided at Bombay that we should procure volunteers through Dattartraya S Parchure [sic] who has already staged a demonstration at Gwalior on or about 24th January 1948.[21]

Savarkar, in his arguments before the court, was careful not to mention any link to Godse or Apte. Eyewitness accounts of the proceedings of the court later mentioned that Savarkar even avoided any conversation or eye contact with the two during the trial and would sit separately from them.

'... after 30th October 1946 there had been no letter sent by Godse to me throughout the years 1947 and 1948,' Savarkar stated in the court.[22] He conveniently forgot that all three had flown together to Delhi on 8 August 1947.

'During the period there was no letter from Apte as well sent to me no letter sent by me to Godse and Apte either singly or jointly [sic]. That means the documentary evidence proves that there was no correspondence whatsoever between us in the years of 1947 or 1948,' Savarkar argued.

> It should be further noted that the Prosecution claims that the alleged conspiracy began somewhere in December 1947 and the Prosecution evidence itself proves as shown above that the Godse Apte correspondence with me ceased more than a year before that period. Consequently, that association too of Godse and Apte with me, which the Prosecution wanted to prove on the strength of that correspondence, must be held to have ceased more than a year before the alleged incubation of the conspiracy as there was no further correspondence to prove its continuance.[23]

The police case that was brought before the court mostly focused on recreating the events that led to Gandhi's assassination, from 10 January 1948 leading up to 30 January 1948. The police had the convenience of the killer confessing to his crime. They barely went into the possibility of a deeper conspiracy in the chargesheet. But to be sure, a lot more evidence and leads were unearthed by the investigation teams regarding the wider network of the conspiracy.

Besides Savarkar and his acolytes, who else would have liked Gandhi dead?

2

Alwar and the Princely Affair

2 February 1948

SOON after the assassination, the police and intelligence agencies started putting the pieces together. The anti-Gandhi rhetoric from Delhi's neighbouring princely state Alwar was too loud to escape the radar of the intelligence bureau. Alwar is barely three hours from Delhi and was a stronghold of the right-wing movement at that time, which received patronage from its Maharaja and his strongman prime minister, Dr Narayan Bhaskar Khare. There were also intelligence reports from Alwar that a godman, a guest of Alwar Municipal Commissioner Giridhar Sharma, had announced that Gandhi was dead at least two hours before the assassination.

Because of this, just two days after the assassination, a police team was dispatched to the state.

Prime Minister N.B. Khare should have been a natural suspect. It was only a few months back, on 12 October 1947, that he had put a 'Brahmin's Curse' on Gandhi.[1] There was also overwhelming evidence of Khare supporting militant Hindu leaders. However, he did not figure in the final charge sheet of the Delhi Police, nor was he indicted by the Jeevan Lal Kapur Commission set up twenty years later. The commission did cast a shadow over the roles of Khare and Alwar state in the conspiracy but gave them the benefit of doubt.

Once again, a key figure in the assassination was let go in absence of 'conclusive evidence'. The commission, in its report, established Khare's role in the following words:

Dr. Khare's antecedents and his encouragement to the R.S.S. and to the militant Hindu Mahasabha leaders were indicative of conditions being produced which were conducive to strong anti-Gandhi activities including a kind of encouragement to those who thought that Mahatma Gandhi's removal will bring about a millennium of a Hindu Raj. But on this evidence the Commission cannot come to the conclusion that there was an active or tacit encouragement to people like Nathuram Godse to achieve the objective of their conspiracy to commit murder of Mahatma Gandhi. But there is no doubt that an atmosphere was being created which was anti-Gandhi even though it may not have been an encouragement to the persons who wanted to murder Mahatma Gandhi.[2]

Did the commission have full access to the material collected by the Delhi Police and the Intelligence Bureau against Khare? The internal investigation documents tell a different story from its report and suggest strong evidence linking Khare's role to Gandhi's assassination.

The godman in question who announced Gandhi's assassination two hours in advance was Gopi Krishna Vyas alias Om Baba. He was the same person Madanlal had mentioned meeting at the Hindu Mahasabha Bhawan ahead of the failed assassination attempt. Om Baba and Madanlal shared Room No. 3 on the night of 19 January after a police car dropped the former at the Hindu Mahasabha Bhawan. He had been in jail for disrupting Gandhi's prayer meeting on 13 January. On that day, when Gandhi had started reciting verses from the Quran, Om Baba chanted Vedic mantras. In police custody, Om Baba began a hunger strike which led to his eventual release.

Room No. 3 is where the dots around the conspiracy of Gandhi's assassination start to get connected to Alwar.

On 7 March, DSP Jaswant Singh wrote a secret note to the director, Intelligence Bureau, and to Inspector General D.W. Mehra:

Ram Singh, an employee of the Hindu Mahasabha Bhawan, Delhi, has been traced today. He states that four or five men (One Hindu Punjabi and four Marhattas) stayed in Room No. 3 of the Hindu Mahasabha Bhawan.

He saw these men on 20.1.1948 and talked with them. These men left the place at about 8 A.M. They again came at 12.00 hours and after a short time they left in a car. He further states that one of them came at about 8. P.M and gave him a chit bearing him address of Poona in Hindi for delivering to one Inder Prakash member of the Hindu Mahasabha. He could not deliver it to Inder Prakash as the latter was not present in the Bhawan ...[3] [sic]

This is the part recorded by Singh in his case diary. His secret note continues:

He further states that a secret meeting took place at Hindu Mahasabha Bhawan 2/3 days before the bomb explosion and Sham Lal Verma, Professor Ram Singh [not the same as the Ram Singh mentioned earlier], Dr. Khere and Mrs. Dr. Khere took part in the meeting. He cannot tell anything about the proceedings of the meeting. Ram Singh states that he can identify all the men who stayed in room No. 3. This Ram Singh claimed to be an ex- I.N.A worker. He was arrested in Chittagong in 1943 and the death sentence was awarded to him on the charge of being 5th columnist but was later on released on appeal.[4] [sic]

It could be that Singh was waiting for directions from his superiors to pursue the lead, but the case diaries show that it was not investigated any further.

✻

Back to Room No. 3. During his stay, Om Baba met Shyam Lal Verma, the editor of a Delhi-based Hindi newspaper, *Singh Nad*. This person was also named by Ram Singh, the servant at the Hindu Mahasabha, as part of the secret meeting ahead of the failed assassination attempt.

On 28 January 1948, Shyam Lal and Om Baba travelled to Alwar by train. Both stayed at Girdhar Sharma's house. On the day of the assassination, according to Om Baba, 'I remember that day he [Shyam Lal] wanted to see the Maharaja of Alwar.'[5]

If this was not enough, an undated interrogation report of Har Lal further independently links those who were mentioned by Ram Singh to the alleged Alwar conspiracy.

Har Lal, a shawl merchant in Old Delhi who was part of the police intelligence network, gave a statement to the Delhi Police in which he said that his business partner Ram Gopal and Har Lal's son had prior knowledge of the assassination. A thorough reading of the statement indicates that Har Lal was trying to exonerate himself and obtain the benefit of doubt for his son. His statement reads as follows: 'I also heard Ram Gopal talk with Om Prakash a few day before the assassination of Mahatma Ji, that Doctor Khare had been arranging for the assassination of Mahatma Ji, and he would know the result very soon that Mahatma Ji would be shot down.'[6] [sic]

The Ram Gopal in question was a leader of the Arya Samaj and a member of the Hindu Mahasabha Working Committee, who was very thick with Professor Ram Singh.

The case diaries related to the investigations show that none of these leads was actively pursued. Which is surprising, considering that M.M.L. Hooja, then deputy director of the Intelligence Bureau who was investigating the Delhi locals for possible links to Gandhi's assassination, said, in a note dated 23 February 1948 to the director of the Intelligence Bureau, that Nathuram Shukla was 'suspected to be the same man as Nathuram Godse.'

During the initial phase of the investigation, as early as 7 February, the probe team in Alwar had concluded that Nathuram Shukla, who was rumoured to be in Alwar ahead of the assassination, was a Hindi journalist. Hooja, who later became director, Intelligence Bureau, was incidentally holding office when the Jeevan Lal Kapur Commission was conducting the re-investigation of the case.

Let us look at the contradictions in the case.

Appearing before the Kapur Commission, Khare was quoted as saying that he 'knew Nathuram Godse only slightly because when he visited Poona as Member of Viceroy's council, Godse came to call on him.'[7]

The word that needs emphasis here is 'slightly'. The report made it sound as if Godse was a distant acquaintance of Khare whom he had met at a function. The commission continued citing Khare in its report: 'He [Khare] did not know that he [Godse] was a leader of the Rashtriya Dal but he did know that he was the editor of the paper *Agrani*.'[8]

Sometimes a simple lie can reveal a lot.

One of the early interrogation reports of Godse recorded him as saying: 'I have never been to Alwar. I had seen in the newspapers that I have been reported to visit Alwar but this is incorrect. I am not acquainted to any of the Hindu Sabha worker of Alwar.'[9] [sic] He thus distanced Khare or any other senior functionaries of Alwar state from being linked to the assassination conspiracy. But his following remarks contradict the public stand taken by Khare:

> But I know Doctor Kharai [Khare], the prime minister of Alwar. The last time I have met Doctor Kharai [Khare] about a year back at Poona when he had met Dr Kharai [Khare] over there. Before this I had met Dr Kharai [Khare] so many times. I had been knowing Doctor Kharai [Khare] because he was a Hindu Sabha leader.[10] [sic]

Clearly, the familiarity between Godse and Khare is much more than 'slight'. It was a relationship that Khare, of course, wanted to hide. But it is intriguing why the investigating officers at the time did not confront both Khare and Godse with the contradictions of their statements, instead of simply accepting their respective versions.

Khare did not just lie about Godse. He claimed no previous association with another accused, Dattatreya Parchure. The Kapur Commission, quoting Khare, stated in its report, 'He did not meet Parchure before 1952 but met him at Gwalior when he went there for election to Parliament. He knew Apte also slightly.'

Nilkantha Dattatreya Parchure, son of Dr Parchure, gave a statement to the police on 15 February 1948: 'Dr N.B. Khare had visited after the last Dusera festival to preside over the Vijaya Lashmi Utsavs and he addressed a meeting stressing the need of Consolidation of the Hindu Rashtra Sangh.'[11] [sic]

The Dusshera of 1947 was on 24 October. This was just a few weeks before Parchure had gone to Bombay and also met with Savarkar and Karkare.

An undated, unsigned statement recorded by the police probe team does not touch on any aspect of the intelligence that was available to them at that time. Going by the content, the two-page statement seems to be a mere formality.

The probe officer recorded:

> I had a talk with Doctor Khare at 11 Cannen Lane, New Delhi, this morning ... he further stated that he does not know anything about any Hindu Rashtriya Dal [sic] whether or not it came to existence in Alwar or in any other place ... He has no knowledge of any posters having been distributed by any Sadhu or a sanyasi in Alwar state. He, however, heard in Alwar on his visit to that place on 4.2.1948 that some police officers from Delhi had been to Alwar and recovered Hindi poster against Mahatma Gandhi.[12]

Right from the beginning, officials of Alwar state were defensive. Inspector Balmukund from the Delhi Police, who was deputed to visit Alwar on 2 February to investigate the incident involving Om Baba announcing Gandhi's murder prior to the actual incident, noted the following conversation with the inspector general of police, Alwar, in his report to his seniors:

The state police would be very glad to give every kind of help to Delhi Police in carrying out the investigation of this case but they would request the Investigation Officer to investigate all the charges against the State people at the spot i.e., at Alwar. They fear that the interested persons from the State may not misguide the Investigating Officer and other high officials by giving them wrong informations.[13] [sic]

The Kapur Commission, while discussing whether Nathuram Shukla was indeed Nathuram Godse, made the following observation that laid out the inherent bias: 'Investigation was unfortunately hampered by the fact that the local police was unreliable and even the I.G.P. was a "staunch Rajput".'[14]

Clearly, the police in Delhi as well as in Alwar were soft on Khare.

*

It was the month of August in 1947 that brought together the different actors who were suspected of planning Gandhi's assassination.

N.B. Khare started the All India Hindu National Front in Delhi in August 1947, which was presided over by Savarkar. It was a meeting of important leaders, including some princes. According to the Kapur Commission reports, Khare couldn't be present at the meeting because of trouble in Alwar. Nor was the Maharaja of Alwar present. However, this does not mean that Khare did not have the opportunity to meet with

Savarkar before the assassination; they met in November 1947 in Bombay.

The Alwar episode raises the question: Why would the princely states want Gandhi assassinated? The answer lies in the views Gandhi expressed in the years closer to Independence.

The first clue ia in a letter Gandhi wrote to Shriman Narayan on 1 December 1945 while on board a train to Calcutta: 'It is worth considering if Pakistan and the Princes can have any place in my conception [of India]. Remember that the Gandhian plan can be successful only if it can be achieved through non-violent means.'[15]

Shriman Narayan was a Gandhian economist and professor in Wardha, the site of Gandhi's ashram Sevagram. He had a longstanding correspondence with Gandhi on several matters, particularly on Gandhian economics. He had even sent the proofs of his book on Gandhian economics to Mahatma Gandhi for his comments.

Gandhi's position vis-à-vis the princes and the princely states is made clearer in his later letters. His letter to Sir Stafford Cripps, who led the Cripps Mission to India in 1942, on 12 April 1946 was a step closer to the hardening stand one observes in his writings ahead of Independence.

Dear Sir Stafford,

What I wanted to say and forgot last night was about the States of India. Pandit Nehru is the President of the States' People's Conference and Sheikh Abdullah of Kashmir its Vice-President. I met the committee of the Conference last Wednesday. Their complaint was that they were ignored by the Cabinet Delegation whereas the Princes were receiving more than their due attention. Of course this may be good policy. It may also be bad policy and morally indefensible. The ultimate result may be quite good, as it must be, if the whole of India becomes independent. It will then be bad to irritate the people of the States by ignoring them. After all the people are everything and the Princes, apart from them, nothing. They owe their artificial status to the Government of India but their existence to the people residing in the respective States. This may be shared with your colleagues or not as you wish. It is wholly unofficial as our talk last night was.

Yours sincerely,
M. K. GANDHI[16]

An expert political strategist, Gandhi's letter to Sir Stafford was no coincidence as the Cabinet Delegation to discuss transfer of power from the British to the Indian leaders, which included Cripps, had arrived in Delhi three weeks ago on 24 March 1946.

With independence in sight, Gandhi's attention was focused on the post-colonial governance. This was also the time that Gandhi was formulating his thoughts on trusteeship, which ran diametrically opposite to the economic interests of the elite, particularly the Hindu elite represented by the princely states.

Before these letters, Gandhi had aired his views on 'trusteeship' in an article about him in *The Hindu* on 9

September 1945, a week after the Second World War ended on 2 September 1945. The war had broken the back of the British empire and it was no secret that the British government was inclined to hand over the reins to India.

> On the question of trusteeship, which was absent from the constitution of the Sangh, Mahatma Gandhi is said to have pointed out that since the theory of trusteeship was stressed by him and had a permanent association with his name, it was legitimate to make it a matter of dispute. He said that he did not want to accentuate class-struggle. The owners should become trustees. They might insist that they should become trustees and yet they might choose to remain owners. We shall then have to oppose and fight them. Satyagraha will then be our weapon. Even if we want a classless society we should not engage in a civil war. Non-violence should be depended upon to bring a classless society.[17]

The Hindu elite, particularly the Hindu Mahasabha, were of the view that the princely states were the custodians of Indian culture. Contrast the Gandhian view, as explicitly expressed in his letter to Narayan, with that of the Hindu Mahasabha, led by Savarkar's effort to strategically position the princely states in the future of India.

Since the electoral debacle for the Hindu Mahasabha in 1937 and the heightened focus on militarization of Hindus, the princely states had become a strategic partner to the Hindu right. In April 1944, the Mahasabha under Savarkar organized three major conferences on the topic of the role of princely states in the idea of India.

Dr Balkrishna Shivram Moonje, Savarkar's close aide and a prominent Mahasabha leader as well as the man leading the efforts to militarize the Hindus, in his presidential address to the Baroda Hindu Sabha in April 1944, one of the three aforementioned conferences, laid out the Mahasabha vision.

The Prince who is ruling the States is a representative of the Hindu Raj of the past and as such incorporates in himself all traditions of dignity and is suffering and fighting for maintaining the Hindu Raj against foreign opponents who were opposing them during the past 500 years or so ... The Hindu Mahasabha therefore calls upon all Hindus to respect and love their Hindu Princes as embodiments of Hindu pride and Hindu achievements in the political world of the past and as hopeful in the future.[18]

The princely state was not a single unit. There was the Prince or Maharaja who was an inheritor of the right to rule and a princely bureaucracy comprising officials such as Khare who had more clout than the inheritor himself. Gandhi correctly identified that the princely bureaucracy was interested in continuing to hold power in a post-colonial structure.

In an article in *Harijan* on 4 August 1946, Gandhi called out the princes but his target was the princely bureaucracy.

As it is, the Princes have taken the lead only in copying the bad points of the British system. They allow themselves to be led by the nose by their Ministers, whose administrative talent consists only in extorting money from their dumb, helpless subjects. By their tradition and training they are unfitted [sic] to do the job you have let them do.[19]

In the mêlée of Hindu-Muslim conflict and the partition politics, an unnoticed war was being waged between Gandhi and the princely states, even as the ideologues of Hindutva courted the princely states, some led by Savarkar and others by Moonje. The ten-year period between 1937 and 1947 saw the perfect marriage between the militant Hindu nationalism of Savarkar–Moonje and the princely states.

Savarkar wrote to the Maharaja of Jaipur on 19 July 1944:

Your Highness must have noted or heard personally from other princes that it was entirely due to my lead that the Hindu Mahasabha as an organization has avowedly embraced a policy of standing by the Hindu states and defending their prestige, stability and power against the Congressites, the Communists, the Moslems and such other internal and external sections who openly declared that they aimed to uproot the Hindu states and encourage every effort to embarrass them and create bad blood between their subjects and themselves. Every Hindu Sabha in a Hindu state is today the only body which takes its stand on the fundamental principle of protecting Hindu states as a part of their duty as Hindus. The Hindu Mahasabha has declared that the Hindu states are centres of Hindu power. The policy carried into effect by my tour of different states succeeded in creating in every Hindu State organised bodies of Hindu Sanghatanists whose loyalty to the State and the Prince was above question.[20]

The essence of this letter portrays—and rightfully so—Gandhi as an arch enemy of the princely states. This conflict escalated closer to Independence. Both Gandhi and the princely states had a different idea about the role of the states in independent India.

In a 26 November 1946 article in *Harijan,* Gandhi was blunt:

It is the people who want and are fighting for independence, not the Princes who are sustained by the alien power even when they claim not to be its creation for the suppression of the liberties of the people. The Princes, if they are true to their professions, should welcome this popular use of paramountcy so as to accommodate themselves to the sovereignty of the people envisaged.[21]

Contrast this stand by Gandhi with that of the Maharaja of Alwar: 'It is the forefathers of the present rulers who have saved India from Muslim domination. The same task lies ahead and we call upon the Hindu Princes to play their rightful role and save the Hindu nation from extinction.'[22]

This appeared as a lead article in the *Hindu Outlook*, the mouthpiece for the Hindu Mahasabha, on 11 March 1947.

Less than a month later, on 4 April 1947, Gandhi, in a one-on-one meeting with Lord Mountbatten, brought up the British strategy of fighting princely states against the Muslim League.

The minutes of the meeting marked 'top secret' stated:

> Mr. Gandhi spoke about the Princes. He said that the Princes were really the creation of the British; that many of them had been gradually created up from small chieftains to the position they now held, because the British realized that they would become strong allies of the British under the system of paramountcy.
>
> In fact he maintained that the British had, from the imperialistic point of view, acted very correctly in backing the Princes and the Muslim League, since between these two, had we played our cards really well, we could have claimed it was impossible for us even to leave India.[23]

By now, Gandhi's position on the princely states had evolved from an opinion to policy and he was convinced enough to see through the intention of the princely states. Gandhi had moral authority and, more importantly, in 1947 with India's upcoming independence, he had success to show. His political communication of using an aspirational language of love and non-violence as against the hate and fear mongering of the Hindutva proponents had a better chance of success. Realistically for most Indians, freedom meant a transfer of power from one ruler to another. But what Gandhi was beginning to talk about had more meaning to their lives that any notional freedom from a foreign power. When Gandhi talked about improving people's lives, providing them with opportunity and creating a more equal and just society, masses were bound to respond favourably. He had already demonstrated his power of political communication with his message of love in Noakhali. (Moonje's frustration in his letter to Sardar Patel has been discussed in the next chapter.)

The princely state and the Hindutva forces were up against Gandhi's powers of communication. Even before the *Hindu Outlook* editorial by the Maharaja of Alwar, Gandhi was systematically reducing the legitimacy of the princely states.

In an interview with Sir M. Derling on 8 April 1947, Gandhi warned Indians of the potential danger posed by the attempts of the princely states to carve out a bigger role for themselves once the British left: '[If the] people of India are not awakened, India will become the battleground for the Princes to fight among themselves and the big ones among them will try to gain sovereignty by swallowing up the smaller ones.'

A close reading of several letters written by Moonje should have helped the Hindutva leadership reach a consensus with Gandhi on this matter. Moonje was looking towards the princely states to fund his dream project of setting up a Hindu military school as the foundation of militarization of the Hindus. It was for this reason that Moonje, in his many letters to the princely states, highlighted the support he was getting from the British Raj. For instance, in his letter to Maharaja Sahib Bahadur Sailana and Alirajpur on 24 July 1936, he said:

> Your Highness, I am sure, will be pleased to know that His Excellency the new Viceroy Lord Linlithgo has set a donation of Rs.250/- with very nice letter of appreciation and goodwill; The new Commander Commander in Chief, Sir Robert Cassels, also has blessed my enterprise and as demonstrable token of his appreciation, sent me a donation of Rs. 100/-.[24] [sic]

He also provided information on the donations received from other princely states as well.

The tone and tenor of Moonje's letters betray his own apprehensions about genuine support if he was unable to convey that the project was not viewed adversely by the British Raj and that other princely states were also supporting it. There were many instances of rich princely states, such as Bikaner and Travancore, showing little interest on account of lack of participation from others. A frustrated letter from Moonje to Maharaja Sahib Bahadur of Bikaner allows a closer insight into this:

> Your Highness was pleased to give me a letter first to H.H. Maharaja Travancore. His Highness first spoke most sympathetically and appreciating and was pleased to remark that Your Highness have already spoken very highly about the scheme of the Military School, which

I am organising. The next question of His Highness was:- What has His Highness Bikaner subscribed? But when it was found that I could not give a direct reply His Highness grew cold and taking leave of me, said that the matter will receive due consideration. [sic]

I had a similar experience once before too about a month ago under similar circumstances H.H. Maharaja Dewas Junior had given me introductions to the smaller Princes of Malwa, but when they found that H.H. Maharaja Dewas had not contributed himself then they grew cold towards me and not much could be done there. [sic]

Letter after letter from Moonje between 1934–37 reflects his frustration about the lack of support from the princely states towards a cause that was central to Hindutva militarization. Yet, after the poor electoral performance during the 1937 elections diminished the political legitimacy of the Hindutva leadership, the princely states provided much-needed backing. It also served the princely states to represent the Hindu cause as this way they could ally themselves with the largest political formation outside of the Congress. Meanwhile, the Congress under the Gandhian influence was moving towards a democratic formation with powers transferred from the princely states to the people.

Gandhi, in the same interview with Derling, gave some unsolicited advice to the princely states with a heavy undertone of potential consequences:

I therefore tell the Princes that they need not have any fears because the Congress has always been in favour of coming to terms with them. The Congress has adopted the policy of non-violence. The Princes have to delegate power to the people's representatives of their own accord. Then the Congress will treat them with respect. We do not want to do away with the Princes. After all, they are also citizens of India, aren't they? The Princes have only to reform themselves and become servants of their subjects. The Congress will be on their side to help them. Unless they mend their ways they will be inviting their own doom.[25]

Gandhi's message of swarajya, or self-rule, was increasingly getting tied into trusteeship.

In his notes to Hiralal Shastri, who later became the prime minister of Jaipur and the first chief minister of Rajasthan (which included the Alwar province), Gandhi gave a call for action: 'If the public is prepared the Princes will themselves see the signs of the times. None of the Princes should be insulted in this connection. The task is to be handled tactfully, lovingly and through persuasion,' he wrote on 20 October 1947.

On 11 November 1947 Gandhi told Shastri,

In free India, the whole country belongs to the people. Not even the smallest portion of it is the private property of the Princes. They can retain their claim only by becoming trustees of the people and that is why they would be required to give evidence of popular support for every action of theirs. True, the Princes have not yet realized that they are the trustees and representatives of the people. And it is also true that with the exception of the alert subjects of some States, the people of all States have not yet realized themselves as the true rulers of their States. But that does not diminish the value of the principle I have laid down.[26]

It ended in almost an ultimatum, 'If the Princes wish to survive, they can do so only as the servants of their people. If they wish to rule, they can do so only as trustees of their people's welfare.'

It was in this context that Khare gave his 'Brahmin Curse' on Gandhi.

The 15 November 1947 All India Congress Committee resolution against the princely states brought the conflict out in the open:

In view of the fact that in a number of States, people's organizations, instead of rising in power and influence as a result of freedom, are being suppressed and prevented from functioning; and further in view of the fact that Rulers in Punjab and some parts of Rajputana and Central India and in the South Indian States have shown an unpatriotic attitude and have betrayed a woeful lack of imagination and have been party to the liquidation of the Muslim and Hindu population by inhuman means, it becomes necessary to reiterate in unequivocal language the policy of the

Congress in regard to the States. Whatever may be the legal implications of accession and lapse of British Paramountcy, the moral result of the independence of India was undoubtedly the establishment and recognition of the power of the people as distinguished from that of Princes and feudal or other interests hostile to natural popular aspirations. This power, the Congress is determined to uphold at any cost. Therefore, all such interests and specially the Princes should know that the Congress cannot uphold them unless they are demonstrably in favour of regarding the voice of the people as the supreme law. In such a democratic State the individual who wants to assert himself against the popular will cannot count, no matter how powerful he may be. This meeting of the A.I.C.C. therefore hopes that the Princes will read the signs of the times and co-operate with the people, and those who have acted in a contrary spirit will retrace their steps and revise their undemocratic conduct and function through democratic organizations expressing the people's will. This they can best do by seeking the association and advice of the A.I.S.P.C. which has been endeavouring to act on behalf of the people of States.[27]

The resolution reflects Gandhi's thought process. There is no doubt in anybody's mind about the influence of Gandhi on the Congress leadership and the government.

During a prayer meeting on 6 January 1948, just weeks before he was assassinated, Gandhi read out a letter:

119

I have a letter from the Maharaja of Aundh, a small State in Maharashtra. He had even when the British rule was still strong in India handed over the reins of the government to the people of his State. He and his son felt that they should serve the people. They devised a constitution, had a body elected and made it responsible for the administration. The Maharaja writes that the feeling among the other Rulers is that whatever he may do he should only do along with the other Rulers and that he should not act all by himself. He has almost decided to merge his State with India but he still continues to be the Raja, though only as a servant of his people. He will accept whatever is sanctioned to him by his people. Sardar Saheb feels that the Rulers should be given pensions, unconditionally.[28]

For any observer, it was a clear message to the princes. It outlined an honourable solution, a subtle threat and an offer.

The princely states and their bureaucracies—which actually held the reins—had not been this close to power in the last five hundred years of Indian history. In fact, many princely states were careful throughout the British rule not to annoy the Raj, with some honourable exceptions in the uprising of 1857; certainly not since the arrival of Gandhi and the mass movement for independence. The princely states and even the Hindutva leadership were preparing for the second coming of the Muslim invaders once the British left. They felt that the burden of preserving the Hindu culture from a foreign assault (read Islamic) lay on their shoulders and therefore were more concerned about being ready to occupy power when the British rule ended.

If the Gandhi assassination probe team was looking for a motive, here it was: revenge for a fatal blow inflicted by Gandhi to a more-than-fifty-year-long grand project of assuming power when the British departure created a vacuum. By ending the legitimacy of princely states, Gandhi did something that even the British had been more considerate about.

3

The Militarization of the Hindus

DR Balkrishna Shivram Moonje has the distinction of playing mentor and disciple, respectively, to two leaders who shaped the militant Hindu identity in India. He was mentor to K.B. Hedgewar, the founder of the RSS, and a disciple and confidant of V.D. Savarkar, the father of Hindutva.

The Moplah rebellion in 1921, as the violent uprising of Muslim peasantry from the Malabar region of Kerala is popularly referred to, had far-reaching consequences. The Muslim leaseholders and cultivators rebelled against Hindu feudal lords who had the patronage of the British Raj.

This was around the time when both Hedgewar and Moonje were making a mark as emerging Hindu leaders. In the aftermath of the Moplah rebellion, the prominent citizens of Nagpur, the city both of them originally belonged to, set up a commission led by Moonje. Its report was finalized in 1923 and concluded that during the rebellion there were cases of forced conversion. It reaffirmed the worst fears of the proponents of Hindutva that the Hindus were ill-prepared for any clash as compared to the Muslims, and that a face-off was imminent. The solution they thought of was to organize Hindus into a militant outfit. Thus, the Moplah rebellion laid the foundation for the mobilization and militarization of Hindus.

The man who was most suited to handle this task of mobilization was Moonje, a practising doctor who had served in the Boer War in South Africa. His commitment towards the militarization of Hindus got a real boost when he visited Europe in the beginning of the 1930s. Moonje took advantage of his visit to London—presumably to attend the Round Table Conferences between 1930 and 1932—to visit military schools in Europe.

On his return, Moonje mooted the idea of setting up a Hindu military school. From 1934, he rallied prominent Hindu businessmen, princes and maharajas to mobilize resources for creating such a school under the aegis of the Hindu Mahasabha.

The application by B.S. Moonje to the executive engineer, Nagpur Division, on 11 April 1934 clearly lays out the aim of the school. This four-page note brings out the fear of an imagined enemy at the gates and his frustration at the divisiveness of the Hindu caste system, which was a deterrent against a unified defence of the motherland from potential aggressors from within and outside.

At its core was the idea of a 'military regeneration of Hindus' by breaking caste barriers, establishing one such school in every province and eventually setting up an All India Military College for training the teachers employed at these institutes.

Moonje's first-hand experience of visiting the areas where the Moplah rebellion had taken place allowed him to reimagine the centuries-old fault lines between Hindus and Muslims. In that light, Moonje identified the Hindu weakness as the single largest threat to Hindus in future.

According to the document:

It is said and also honestly felt by many who have witnessed and carefully analysed the results of the Hindu Muslim disturbance during the last four or five years that the Hindu cannot defend themselves even in places where they preponderate in numbers. To give them adequate protection, police and sometimes auxiliaries and even British soldiers have to be drafted. They argue that if this is still so in internal Indian domestic communal disturbances, how well then the majority community, the Hindus, be considered fit to undertake the responsibility of national defence rallied from foreign aggression which is, they say, the first test to prove if India is fit for the dominion status. Thus they argue that the state of Hindu weakness is the greatest obstacle in the way of Swaraj.[1]

In a critique of Gandhi's non-violence, the document cited Sir Denys Bray, the foreign secretary to the government of India. In order to give an unbiased comparison of the 'military quotient' of Hindus versus Muslims, Moonje gave a lot of emphasis to

Bray's experience of two regions—the Hindus of Hindustan on one side and the Afghans and Pathans of Afghanistan and the Trans-Frontier Country on the other. He quoted Bray's farewell address at the Chelmsford Club on 23 December 1929:

There is one practical lesson my long work at the Foreign Office has seared across my brain—In the idea of complete independence as Indians goal there is in theory, no doubt, something logical and therefore superficially something most attractive even to a man like myself; but until a lamb and a lion lie down together and the lion never opens his jaws except to recite the Kellogg pact to the admiring lamp, complete independence is a mirage, a treacherous luring of India——India is therefore still in need of generous and adventurous youths of England in her service.[2]

Surely, for the British, the idea of a military school held great appeal. In a letter dated 17 November 1935, Field Marshal Philip Walhouse Chetwode who, like Moonje, had served in the British Indian army during the Boer's War and was sympathetic to the 'Indianization' of the Indian army, wrote:

It gives me great pleasure to support your efforts in endeavouring to start a Public School near Nagpur, in the Central Provinces. I am quite certain that, from an Army point of view, we shall never get that constant supply of young men which is essential for the Army unless more and more Public Schools are started in

India; and I can only hope that the one in which you are personally interested will set an example that will be followed all over the country.

I have pleasure in enclosing a donation for Rs 100.[3]

In a separate letter on the same day, he assured Moonje of a reference to his successor, Sir Robert Cassels: 'I am leaving your requests with my personal Military Secretary, to place before General Sir Robert Cassels, the new Commander-in-Chief, and I feel sure that he will do all he can to help you.'

These letters were followed by an in-person meeting between the two on 15 November 1935 at 11.30 a.m.

To be sure, General Cassels as well as Viceroy Lord Linlithgow supported the idea with a token donation of 250 rupees each. Besides having served as an officer in the medical corps, Moonje had been making representations to increase the intake of Indian officers in order to 'Indianize' the army. In 1926, the Skeen Committee validated Moonje's demand and promised that Indians would constitute 50 per cent of the Indian army by 1952.

During his visit to London to attend the First Round Table Conference from November 1930 to January 1931, Moonje visited military schools in Italy. The Balilla and Avanguardist organizations there were responsible for the military training and fascist indoctrination of underaged boys.

Moonje identified the reinvention of the martial instinct in Hindus as the urgent need. According to him, it had been compromised because of the practice of non-violence for centuries, caste-driven deployment and lack of a Hindu political consciousness. The only way to address this was to inculcate a sense of emergency and a self-critical awareness of their weaknesses. It was almost as if the only way to unite Hindus was to identify a common enemy and recognize the imminent threat from it.

Moonje elaborated this 'crisis of Hindus' in the general scheme of the Hindu Mahasabha Military School that he submitted for setting it up:

Looking at present condition of Hindus from the point of view, it cannot be denied that physical development of a boys is at a low ebb have an emotional instinct is practically extinct in most of them. All our effort should, therefore, be concentrated on reviving the martial instinct and making them fit both physically and mentally for self-defence. The Hindus form a large majority of the population and being caste-ridden required to be trained with special care and attention— to fit them to take their due share in accordance with the numbers in the defence of the country, as compared with the Moslems who from the socio-religious point of view, are more favorably situated in—this respect, being unencumbered with the well-known handicaps of the caste-system. Every able-bodied young Mohammed therefore is a political soldier, and as such a little training is enough to make him fit to fight more efficiently than an average Hindu can do. But that is not the case with Hindus who have a caste system ingrained in them which makes the duty of fighting obligatory on one caste alone, i.e the Kshatriya caste. The Kshatriya alone as a caste has been trained to fight, while the Brahmans, the Vyashas and the Sudras have been regarded as not being required to fight. But the form more than three-fourths of the Hindu population and they have been by the tradition of long ages weaned away as if it were from the profession of war. The latent martial capacity in them, though shining out with equal glamour in exceptional cases, has not yet been generally quickened. The Hindus, therefore, in any emergency will not be able to supply soldiers for the defense of the motherland in the same proportion as a Muslim can in proportion to their numbers. Besides, speaking from a larger point of view, no movement for Swaraj could be said to be soundly based where the—largest and most influential community, the Hindus is designated as non-martial. Thus, in the case of the Hindus a special effort is needed to instill into their mind the spirit of warfare and to develop their bodies in a scientific way for the purpose. The time has come when the English people alone would not be able to defend India in times of emergency without the trained co-operation of Indians. The question therefore before the Hindu Mahasabha is how to quicken the latent martial spirit of the Hindus and how to arrange to give them suitable training with the object of making them fit to undertake and shoulder the entire responsibility of the defense of India as the exigencies of the political situation may at anytime dictate.[4] [sic]

What Do Hindus Have to Defend?

The Hindutva ideologues felt a need to defend the motherland. The architecture of the Hindu Military School in Nasik, also known as Bhonsala Military School—named after one of the early donors to the project, the Bhonsala royal family—is the most appropriate metaphor to explain the Hindu militarization project and its objective.

The octagon-shaped school complex with a temple at the centre has eight gates. 'These gates have been variously named. The ideology behind the selection of these names is to bring out the inspiring age-old History of our forefathers in a concrete form and to impress it on the virgin, sensitive and responsive minds of our raw boys and girls,' Moonje said in the preface to the general scheme.[5]

The school complex is perhaps the first symbol of the motherland, Bharatvarsha or Hindustan, which means the land of the children of King Bharat, the land of the Hindus.

'From the historical fact, it will be clear that, having regarded the site of the School as the replica in miniature of this vast land of Hindustan, it is in the fitness of things that this site has been named the "Rama-Bhoomi".'[6]

The gates of the school represent the boundaries of India and indicate the directions in which they were expanding and the direction through which the early Muslim invaders entered. They are meant to be a daily reminder of the land the students have to defend and protect for the sake of Hindustan.

The northern gate was called the Hindu Kush Gate. The name referred to the original boundary of India that extended beyond the mountains of Kabul and Kandahar, once known as Hindu Kush Mountains. It acted as a reminder that the then international border, the Durand Line between Afghanistan and Pakistan, was only as recent as 1893, a result of the Second Anglo-Afghan war.

The northwest gate was a sordid reminder of the invasions of Mahmud of Ghazni and was named the Afghanistan Gate. The ransacking of the Somnath Temple in Gujarat by Ghazni was still considered a blot on Hindu masculinity. Also, for Maharashtrians, it was a matter of pride since it was the Marathas who had ended Muslim rule with the battle of Panipat against Aurangzeb.

The Persian Gulf Gate on the western side symbolized the direction from which the Arabs first invaded India.

The eastern gate, called the Burma-Japan Gate, was symbolic of the eastward expansion of the Hindu culture and religion in Burma (now Myanmar), China and Japan. The northeast gate, called the Nepal Gate, was in celebration of the last Hindu kingdom.

The southern gate was called the Kanyakumari Gate, named after the southernmost limit of India. The southwest gate, known as the Aden-Arabia Gate, indicated where the Europeans had invaded India through the sea route. The Jagannatha Puri Gate in the southeast celebrated the casteless represented within the eponymous temple compound. It also celebrated Hindu valour by serving as a reminder of the brave albeit unsuccessful defence by Hindus of the temple against the eighteen attacks on it by the Mughals, particularly Aurangzeb.

The buildings on the sides of these gates were also dedicated to eight heroes and heroines who had defended the integrity of Hindustan at various points. These were meant to inspire the young cadets, called Ramadandees, meaning the holders of the danda or sceptre of Rama.

Militarization provides an opportunity for ritual, which binds collective memory and purpose. It is one way to organize a disunited society. For the Hindutva brigade, it was symbolic, somewhat like the charkha, which Gandhi effectively used as a symbol of defiance and self-reliance. In the case of the militarization project, it combined both symbols and rituals and made them more powerful. The human mind can develop a strong attachment if high principles are connected to memory and symbols and people's sense of history. The collective imagination can always be shaped. Here the militarization of Hindus combined self-honour with the idea of India as defined by these eight sides and a ritual that built camaraderie. It gave purpose to the lives of the cadets and broke down the pre-existing biases and boundaries within the larger Hindu community.

'Signor Mussolini, they say, never forgets. We also want our boys never to forget the obligations of their own history. It is this purpose that has inspired the conception of this kind of a layout,' Moonje explained in the bulletin which laid out the philosophy of the school complex architecture.[7]

The militarization of Hindus followed the same adage: never forget your past, never lower your guard and always be ready to defend your country against any imminent threat.

We must also equally learn the lesson of History that the Western and Northwestern gates of the Himalayas must never again be violated at any point by enemy armies of foreign people.

We must also, as preached by Signor Mussolini, cultivate the means to frustrate any attempt at their violation in future that is to grow strong; so that nations like England on one side and Afghanistan on the other, maybe friendly with us. We must study and assimilate the Science and Art of warfare of Europe and cultivate the European mentality of Militarism and Diplomacy which alone will guarantee immunity from such violations.[8]

The foundational document prepared by Moonje in 1934 summarizes the Hindu Mahasabha's need for militarization: 'Thus for the Hindu Mahasabha the entire question has been simplified. In order to attain Swaraj and to maintain it when attained, the Hindu Mahasabha has to see that the Hindus are not and do not remain lambs; they have, therefore, to be made tigers.'[9]

In 1947, the time to fight for India and protect her from an imminent threat of Muslim takeover once the British left had come. But the single-largest threat to this long-awaited judgement day for which the Hindu Mahasabha had been preparing was the old fakir, Mahatma Gandhi. The Hindu Mahasabha leaders, including Savarkar, always maintained that Gandhi's doctrine of non-violence would lead the Hindus to a genocide at the hands of Muslims, for they did not subscribe to it.[10]

The ability of Gandhi to sabotage the ambitious project of a Hindu resurgence was real. He had shown his might in the riot-torn Noakhali in Bengal in 1946, where his fast unto death had stopped violence. But the Hindus were not fully avenged for the massive violence that had resulted in disproportionate loss to the Hindu side.

Moonje's letter to Sardar Vallabhbhai Patel, then home minister and a diehard Gandhian, on 6 January 1947, betrays the worst fears of the Hindu Mahasabha about Gandhi, the pacifier coming in the way of an emasculated Hindu defending his motherland and women from the Muslim aggressor. The letter was written in the context of the arrest of 1,400 Hindus, alleged rioters in Bihar.

When I was in Bihar, I had personally noted how the people felt the sting of Mahatma Gandhi's accusation against them that they were a disgrace to humanity. They felt distressed and disappointed because in the heart of hearts, they felt and knew that they were really not the aggressors and that though the Moslems were really the aggressors even in Bihar. They were feted and treated as if they were the honourable guests of the Government. Such discrimination was causing great demoralization amongst the Hindus. Would such a demoralization, if cause, pay the Congress Government, that is, the Hindu Government in the long run?

... It is now certain that the Hindu-Moslem question will not be settled without war. Mr. Churchill is at the bottom and Mr. Jinnah will not give it at least until the next General Elections in England.

... Under the circumstances, I feel that we Hindus will be no where if the Hindu masses are thus subjected to demoralization when the real testing time of the bloody war between the Hindus and Moslems come.

... But after all is retaliation a crime? ... retaliation is human nature and no moral crime.[11]

If there was one real question that could not be publicly discussed in the upcoming Working Committee of the All India Hindu Mahasabha ahead of 15 August 1947 and the partition of India as drawn out by Cyril Radcliffe, it was: how to stop Gandhi?

In Book 1, Chapter 1, the evidence that the key conspirators of Gandhi's assassination were present in New Delhi in August 1947 was laid out. Savarkar attended the Working Committee meeting of the All India Hindu Mahasabha after a gap of three years.

The minutes of the meeting of the Mahasabha on the inaugural day, 9 August 1947, noted that 'Veer Savarkar took a leading part in the discussion at the Committee.'[12]

The meeting was also attended by Moonje, among other stalwarts of the Mahasabha.

But what went down in the meeting was a bitter discussion about two things of historical significance. Firstly, for the Hindu Mahasabha, India's independence was not an occasion for celebration; rather, it was a sorrowful moment because of the creation of Pakistan.

> The committee was of [the] opinion that Hindu Mahasabhaits should not associate themselves with or participate in the rejoicings that are being organized by the Congress for the 15th August will bring into being also a 2nd independent state called Pakistan within the territories of India a which is much more a matter for sorrow and heart searching than for rejoicings.[13] [sic]

Secondly, the new flag of independent India was not acceptable to the Mahasabha, which wanted a Bhagwa Flag, once adopted by Chhatrapati Shivaji and a symbol of Hindu nationalism.

> Though the flag devised by such an assembly cannot be accepted as a National Flag, the working committee was nevertheless of the opinion that no disrespect should be shown either to the state flag or to any party flag. The committee decided to hold public meetings on 15th August and to hoist Bhagwa Flag and to take a formal oath in public meetings expressing their determination for reunification of India.[14]

For the Hindu Mahasabha, India's independence was an unfinished project. The most vociferous political opponent to the Mahasabha's idea of India was none other than the old fakir, Mahatma Gandhi.

Book III
The Fakir

1

Imagined Enemies

ON 12 December 2019, the central government of India enacted the Citizenship (Amendment) Act, 2019. The following clause was added to the original act of 1955:

> Provided that any person belonging to Hindu, Sikh, Buddhist, Jain, Parsi or Christian community from Afghanistan, Bangladesh or Pakistan, who entered into India on or before the 31st day of December, 2014 and who has been exempted by the Central Government by or under clause (c) of sub-section (2) of section 3 of the Passport (Entry into India) Act, 1920 or from the application of the provisions of the Foreigners Act, 1946 or any rule or order made thereunder, shall not be treated as illegal migrant for the purposes of this Act.[1]

In many ways, the exercise of updating the National Register of Citizens (NRC) in Assam, which began in 2015 and concluded in August 2019, was a precursor to the CAA legislation. The 'illegal Muslims infiltrating' into India from Bangladesh (and Myanmar) were the targets. Nineteen lakh Indians were declared 'stateless' after this; 1.08 lakh D-voters (doubtful voters) were barred from voting in the 2021 Assam elections. The CAA legislation was passed in December 2019, right on the heels of the release of the NRC list. The omission of the Muslim community in the amended Citizenship Act was a deliberate move. When many parts of the country erupted in non-violent civil rights protests, the state swiftly doubled down on the dissenters. From 'who is an Assamese', the question of citizenship snowballed into 'who is an Indian.'

These anxieties about who really is an Indian are not at all new; Savarkar repeatedly fanned them in his writings and fused them into his idea of Hindutva. In his popular book, 'Essentials of Hindutva', Savarkar makes a fanciful if somewhat dense case for who is a true 'son' of Hindustan. Like a good barrister, Savarkar prepared a list of qualifications essential to be a Hindu and defined who could lay claim to this motherland or the matribhu. The first of these is geographical—the Hindu is a citizen by birth or by the birth of his forefathers. He lays claim to the motherland himself or through his patriarchs, and thus it also becomes his fatherland, or pitribhu.

The second condition is that a true Hindu should be a descendant of Hindu parents; in his veins should flow the sanskriti of Sindhu. The son of the soil is the offspring of Hindu dharma of all shades, Vedic and non-Vedic, of Buddha, Jain, or 'any extremely modern ones of Chaitanya, Chakradhar, Basava, Nanak, Dayananda or Raja Rammohan'. He should be such a perfect embodiment of the culture and philosophy of Hindus that Hindusthan becomes not just his matribhu and pitribhu but also the punyabu or the holy land. He who looks upon the land that extends from the Sindhu [Indus river] to the Sindhu [ocean in Sanskrit]—Bharatbhumi—as his birthplace or matribhu, the land of his forefathers or pitrubhu, and his holy land or punyabu, is a true Hindu.[2]

Savarkar's conception of the nation and its citizens is a selective anamnesis of the past, in which not all inhabitants of the land feature. His Bharatbhumi is the land of the 'founders of our faith, 'the seers to whom "veda" was revealed, from vaidik seers to Dayananda, from Jina to Mahavir, from Buddha to Nagasen, from Nanak to Govind, from Banda to Basava, from Chakradhar to Chaitanya, from Ramdas to Rammohan'. This is the land, he says, where the gurus and godmen were born and lived.

Here Bhagirath rules, there Kurukshetra lies. Here Ramchandra made his first halt of an exile, there Janaki saw the golden deer and fondly pressed her lover to kill it. Here the divine Cowherd played on his flute that made every heart in Gokul dance in harmony as if in a hypnotised sleep. Here is Bodhi Vriksha, here the deer-park, here Mahaveer entered Nirvana. Here stood crowds of worshippers amongst whom Nanak sat and sang the Arati ... Here Gopichand the King took on vows of Gopichand the Jogi and with a bowl in his hand knocked at his sister's door for a handful of alms! Here the son of Bandabahadur was hacked to pieces before the eyes of his father and the young bleeding heart of the son thrust in the father's mouth for the fault of dying as a Hindu! Every stone here has a story of martyrdom to tell! Every inch of thy soil, O Mother! has been a sacrificial ground! So to every Hindu, from the Santal to the sadhu this Bharata bhumi, this Sindhustan is at once a Pitribhu and a Punyabu—fatherland and a holy land.[3]

In May 1921, Vinayak Damodar Savarkar's ten-year imprisonment at the Cellular Jail in the Andamans came to an end. Onboard the SS *Maharaja*, the Savarkar brothers— Vinayak and Babarao—docked in at Calcutta and were later transferred to the district prison in Ratnagiri. In 1922, looking at the developments of the Khilafat agitation, the civil disobedience movement and the Moplah riots, Savarkar composed his magnum opus *Essentials of Hindutva*, which he claimed was an intellectual response formulating the idea of Hindu identity. This work became central to building the ideology of Hindutva. In 1946, more than two decades after *Essentials of Hindutva* was published, the All India Hindu Mahasabha outlined the definition of a 'Hindu' who alone can seek membership to the Sabha, bearing close resemblance to Savarkar's idea of who is a Hindu.

A person who permanently regards or adopts in word and deed this Bharatvarsa from the Sindhus to the seas [from the Himalayas to the seas] only as this fatherland [or homeland] as well as his only Holy land, both culturally and nationally, and who does not retain, or, except by compulsion, in fact under any extra-territorial allegiance [of any kind] is a Hindu. (The word does not signify any religion or religious group of people).

a)   A person who cannot call himself a 'Hindu' [in the above sense] is not a Hindu or is a Non-Hindu, and as such cannot be a member of Hindu Mahasava.

Explanation: Permanently—not   temporarily   or conveniently for ulterior use; adopts—e.g. persons of foreign origin or allegiance, only (Fatherland)— (excluding dual idea & psychology); only (Holy land)— excluding dual regard;
   Culturally—refers to standard of morality and ethics; nationally—territorial patriotism;

1. (a) is separate—it does not exclude any community and as such does not render Hindu Mahasava a Communal body, but indicates that a declaration is necessary for membership.[sic][4]

A similar narrative has made its way to the present day in the form of a register and a legislation (CAA-NRC), which claim not to be communal but actively leave out people who don't meet the conditions of their enclosed definition.

   Savarkar's idea of the nation is circumscribed by Hindu religion; in his definition, the true citizens of this land are essentially Hindus—which encompasses Buddhists, Jains and Sikhs. These ideas are the seeds for the growth of a theocratic state, not a republic.

In his book *The Discovery of India*, Jawaharlal Nehru writes about a different idea of the nation:

> ...all of us I suppose, have varying pictures of our native land and no two persons will think exactly alike. When I think of India, I think of many things: of broad fields dotted with innumerable villages; of towns and cities I have visited; of the magic of the rainy season which pours life into the dry parched-up land and converts it suddenly into a glistening expanse of beauty and greenery; of great rivers and flowing waters; of the Khyber Pass in all its bleak surroundings; of the southern tip of India; of people, individually and in the mass; above all, of the Himalayas ...We make and preserve pictures of our choice.[5]

The contention here is not about which idea of India is accurate; rather, our argument is that the Savarkarite conception does not allow for the differences that animate and enrich this land. One single idea cannot encapsulate what it is to belong to this nation; whereas the Savarkarite nation is an unchangeable, fixed entity enclosed by a religion that claims dominance in the land.

It is not far-fetched, then, to assume that the roots of the CAA legislation or a register of citizens lie in Savarkar's idea of the nation and who its true claimants are. Savarkar himself makes this clear:

> That is why in the case of some of our Mohammedan or Christian countrymen who had originally been forcibly converted to a non-Hindu religion and who consequently have inherited along with Hindus, a common Fatherland and a greater part of the wealth of a common culture—language, law, customs, folklore and history—are not and cannot be recognized as Hindus. For though Hindusthan to them is Fatherland as to any other Hindu yet it is not to them a holy land too. Their holy land is far off in Arabia or Palestine. Their mythology and Godmen, ideas and heroes are not the children of this soil ... Their love is divided. We are not condemning nor are we lamenting. We are simply telling the facts as they stand.[6]

A common nation (rashtra), a common race (jati) and a common civilization (sanskriti)—these are the essentials of Hindutva. In modern-day India, this has translated into 'one nation, one culture.' A 'handy' definition of this, penned by Savarkar, reads, 'A Sindu Sindhu paryanta, Yasya Bharatbhumika Pitribhuh Punyabhushchaiva sa vai Hinduriti smritah', meaning, a Hindu is one for whom Sindhusthan is both a fatherland and holy land. Hindutva equates being Hindu to being a citizen of India and, by doing so, condemns the Muslims and Christians of the land to the fate of stateless 'illegal foreigners.'

Other than Hindutva and who/what is a Hindu, the other preoccupation in Savarkar's writings is an enduring hostility to the practice of ahimsa or non-violence. It is no secret that Mahasabhites as well as other Hindutva ideologues and revolutionaries bitterly resented Mahatma Gandhi's constant adherence to ahimsa. They felt that the principle of non-violence was impractical and had resulted in the weakening of Hindu masculinity. History was witness to this as well. In Savarkar's perception of history, the rise and fall of Buddhism is central to understanding Hindus' relationship with violence and non-violence. Buddhists went out into the world to spread the word about their religion as well as the land they inhabited. Suddenly, the international profile of India became active. Outsiders, Savarkar writes, began to knock at our door more impudently than they ever had done. Pilgrims, scholars, teachers, travellers, saints and sages began to pour into the land; Bharat came to be known as Sindhu or Hindu. Buddhism brought India into contact with the world. When Buddhism declined in India, the world came even closer to the land of Sindhu, with disastrous consequences for the inhabitants, he writes. 'The political consequences of the Buddhistic expansion have been so disastrous to the national virility and even the national existence of our race.'[7] The practice of ahimsa in Buddhism had rendered India so weak that it became an easy prey to war-mongering tribes like the Huns. While Buddhists held onto their practice of non-violence, their hymns and chants, the Hindus were unable to stomach the barbaric violence they faced from the invaders. '[The] rest of the Hindus could not drink with equanimity this cup of bitterness and political servitude.'

Buddhism may have put us on the world map, and that too for the ideology of ahimsa, but Savarkar argued that the Hindu nation had achievements beyond those of the Buddhist Bhikkus. He said that the 'political virility and manly nobility of our race' did not begin or end with the rise and fall of Buddhism. In *Essentials of Hindutva*, Savarkar made an argument that Nathuram Godse repeated when he criticized Gandhi's belief in ahimsa in his final denouement at the Red Fort murder trial. Buddhism has conquests to claim, Savarkar said, but they are far removed from the real world and its practicalities, 'where feet of clay do not stand long, and steel could be easily sharpened, and thirst is too powerful and real to be quenched by painted streams that flow perennially in heavens.' When nomadic tribes invaded India, 'like volcanic torrents and burnt all that thrived', Indians saw their lands being looted, their gods being trampled upon, their holy land plundered by invaders who were 'so inferior to them in language, religion, philosophy, mercy, and all the soft and human attributes of man and god—but superior to them in strength alone—strength that summed up its creed in two words—Fire and Sword!' For the Hindus, it became clear that the Buddhist practice could not vanquish this new and terrible foe. Ahimsa had to be shunned, the sacrificial fires had to be rekindled, the Vedic mines of steel had to be reopened to drive away the foreigner. 'Back to the Vedas' was a cry that became a political necessity for protection and survival, according to Savarkar.[8]

For a while, Hindus were lulled into a sense of false security, until Mahmud of Ghazni crossed the Indus to invade Sidhusthan. At this juncture, faced with an Islamic invader, Savarkar writes:

> ... nothing makes Self conscious of itself so much as a conflict with non-self. Nothing can weld peoples into a nation and nations into a state as the pressure of a common foe. Hatred separates as well as unites. Never had Sindhusthan a better chance and a more powerful stimulus to be herself forged into an indivisible whole as on that dire day, when the great iconoclast crossed the Indus.[9]

This lies at the heart of Hindutva and Hindu masculinity. They are ideas and states of being defined by the 'other'.

In impassioned, persuasive prose—but without giving any sources at all—Savarkar writes that India was invaded by not just one or two races or tribes, but nearly all of Asia, including Arabs, Pathans, Persians, Baluchis, Turks and Mughals, followed by nearly all of Europe. Religion, in this case Islam, combined with 'rapine' wreaked havoc and devastation, and brought misery on Sindhusthan. Mahmud of Ghazni especially carried out one such conquest that took India by surprise. 'Day after day, decade after decade, century after century, the ghastly conflict continued,' Savarkar writes. This conflict ended when the last of the Mughals was dethroned. In this retelling of history, it is clear that the Muslim replaced the British as the enemy for proponents of Hindutva. The Hindu consciousness was intensely felt by Hindus as a whole and was 'welded into a nation to an extent unknown in our history', when faced with the Muslim 'other'.

The Hindu self that is forged when faced by the 'other' encompasses all creeds, castes and sects of Hinduism. This articulation of Hindu includes 'Sikhs, Sanatanis, Marathas and Madrasis'—'all suffered as Hindus and triumphed as Hindus'. From Attock (in Pakistan) to Cuttack (in India), the Hindu became one single being. 'This one word, Hindutva, ran like a vital spinal cord through our whole body politic and made the Nayars of Malabar weep over the sufferings of the Brahmins of Kashmir', writes Savarkar.[10]

To summarize, the elements of Hindutva and therefore being Indian are spelled out clearly by Savarkar: one can call themselves a citizen of India only if their loyalty is to this motherland, they as well as their forefathers are born here— making this their fatherland—and they call this their holy land. The Hindu is not a believer in non-violence like his Buddhist ancestors. In the face of (ever-imminent, however imaginary) Islamic aggression and invasion, Hindutva is the spinal cord that runs across the body politic of Hindus to unite them across all lines of division. In a 1990 essay, at a time when the Berlin Wall had fallen and the dissolution of the Soviet Union was underway, Slavoj Žižek wrote about the 'gradual retreat of liberal-democratic tendency in the face of corporate national populism...'. As Žižek argues:

National identification is by definition sustained by a relationship towards the Nation qua Thing ... It appears to us as 'our Thing' as something only accessible to us, as something 'they', the others, cannot grasp, but that is nonetheless constantly menaced by 'them'. It appears as what gives plenitude and vivacity to our life, and yet the only way we can determine it is by resorting to different versions of an empty tautology ...[11]

How do we recognize this concept of nation—we point to its presence in this elusive thing called 'our way of life'. In Savarkar's conception, Hindutva constituted 'our way of life', whereas the Gandhian conception foregrounded non-violence and morality.

2

The Idea of Hindutva

O N 15 December 2019, two weeks after the Citizenship (Amendment) Act was passed in Parliament, students of Jamia Millia Islamia university in Delhi came under attack by the Delhi Police for holding protests against the legislation. Students across universities in India rose up in anger at the state, including at the Indian Institute of Technology (IIT), Kanpur. They sang Pakistani poet Faiz Ahmed Faiz's universal protest anthem *'Hum Dekhenge'.* Less than a month later, the institution set up a formal inquiry to look into a complaint raised against the recital of the Urdu poem; the complaint claimed that Faiz's anthem provoked anti-Hindu sentiments. In particular, the lines *'Jab arz-e-Khuda ke Ka'abe se, sab but uthwaae jaayenge/ Hum ahl-e-safa mardood-e-haram, masnad pe bithaaye jaayenge/ Sab taaj uchhale jaayenge, sab takht giraaye jaayenge'* (From the abode of God, when the icons of falsehood will be removed/ When we, the faithful, who have been barred from sacred places, will be seated on a high pedestal/ When crowns will be tossed, when thrones will be brought down).[1]

The complaint and the subsequent formal inquiry caused a stir in the public domain, especially at a time when tensions were already heightened. The left and liberal commentariat defended Faiz as an atheist and a communist who had taken artistic licence with Islamic imagery. The poem, many argued, was a powerful indictment of dictatorship in Pakistan at the time it was written and a call to restore democracy and return power to the oppressed. These explanations, however accurate, did not satisfy the Hindus, who were offended and complained. It did not matter that Faiz Ahmed Faiz was a staunch communist. It did not matter that the right-wing interpretation was too literal and taken wholly out of context. What mattered was that *'Hum Dekhenge'* had a reference to 'murti bhanjan', i.e., the destruction of idols—*sab but uthwaeye jayenge*—this was a longstanding source of hatred and discontent for Hindus. Why was a communist poet's rallying cry against authoritarianism and oppression construed as a direct attack on the Hindu religion?

The clues to this perhaps lie in understanding the Hindu nationalist interpretation of the history of the subcontinent. To be a Savarkarite Hindu, one who conforms to Hindutva—one nation, one jati, one sanskriti—is to be a Hindu burdened by the past. This Hindu carries scars that seemingly cannot be healed; their hatred towards the enemy is irreversible, fuelled by a variety of anxieties. To return to the controversy around *'Hum Dekhenge'* and what it really signified, we must go back nearly a thousand years.

In 1026, Mahmud of Ghazni raided the Somnath Temple in present-day Gujarat and destroyed the temple idol, sparking antagonistic relations between Hindus and Muslims that continue to this day. Remember that Bharatiya Janata Party (BJP) leader Lal Krishna Advani began the Ram Janmabhoomi rath yatra from Somnath on 25 September 1990, setting off a chain of events that ended with the demolition of the Babri Masjid in Ayodhya in 1992 and the resulting communal violence. In the nationalist Hindu's retelling of the past, Muslim iconoclasm such as Mahmud's raid has become a central preoccupation and the Somnath Temple is its most important symbol.

The Somnath episode was invoked by Swami Sampurnanand Saraswati, an Arya Samaj leader, in his introduction to Savarkar's fictionalized account of the Moplah riots. The 1921–22 revolt was significant for many reasons—first, Muslims replaced the British as the primary enemy for Savarkar and the Hindu Mahasabha, and second, Hindu Mahasabhites began to identify Mahatma Gandhi with Muslim appeasement in the aftermath of the Khilafat movement and the Moplah rebellion. In his preface to Savarkar's *'Moplah, arthart mujhe isse kya?'* (What does Moplah mean to me?), the Arya Samaji holds two central features of Hinduism responsible for its ruination—casteism and idol worship. The latter, he writes, is responsible for multiple wars with Islam. In his retelling, while Mahmud of Ghazni plundered the Somnath Temple for its wealth, Kshatriya warriors and Brahmin priests waited for an auspicious time.

Once the temple was surrounded by Mahmud's forces, they capitulated or fled. A sum of three crore rupees was offered to the invading forces in exchange for the temple idol, which they declined. Mahmud of Ghazni and his army told the temple guardians that they were iconoclasts (butpurast not butshikan) and proceeded to smash the idol, taking with them precious gemstones worth eighteen crore rupees. Sampurnanand wrote that invading Muslim armies destroyed Hindu gods, time and time again, making them weak, craven and small in front of Islam. Muslim iconoclasm over centuries crushed the willpower and morale of the Hindus.

Of course, this story is not moored to historical evidence. Out of the 60,000-odd instances of temple destruction by Muslim rulers cited by Hindutva sources, Richard Eaton, a well-known historian, contends that only eighty instances have reasonably certain historicity. He also points out that iconoclasm was not the exclusive preserve of Muslim rulers, as Hindutva would like to argue; there is evidence of numerous instances where Hindu kings have torn down Hindu temples, even Jain and Buddhist shrines. The acts of temple destruction ought to be seen for what they were— powerful political strategies—and not as deliberate acts of communal violence.[2]

Historian Romila Thapar tells us about different versions of the events that transpired at the Somnath Temple in 1026 that make it somewhat difficult to ascertain whether or not Mahmud Ghazni actually destroyed the temple idols.

In 1919, Indian Muslims began a pan-Islamist political movement to restore the Caliphate of the Ottoman Empire, called the Khilafat Movement. This campaign was bolstered by Mahatma Gandhi's simultaneous call for the non-cooperation movement. Gandhi became a crucial link between the two movements, pivoting a national campaign on Hindu–Muslim unity. In fact, the Ali brothers (Shaukat Ali and Mohammad Ali Jauhar), who were the leaders of the Khilafat agitation, led the first national call for non-cooperation. The Khilafat leaders were so keen to get the backing of the Hindu political leadership that they offered to give up the slaughter of cows on Bakr-Id (in the 1911 Muslim League resolution). In 1920, the Hunter Commission report on the Jallianwala Bagh massacre was published; Michael O'Dwyer, the then lieutenant governor of Punjab, was acquitted and Colonel Reginald Dyer, the 'butcher of Amritsar', let off without so much as a censure. The Treaty of Sevres was also signed that year, which led to the collapse of the Ottoman Empire. The time was ripe for the non-cooperation movement to be launched and Gandhi pushed for the campaign to focus on the issues of 'Khilafat wrong', 'Punjab wrong', and 'Swaraj'. The non-violent resistance called for the boycott of titles, civil services, police and army, and for the non-payment of taxes. However, the Khilafat agitation spread to smaller towns and began to acquire different forms and meanings. The most significant offshoot was seen in Malabar, Kerala, where Muslim tenants rose up against their Hindu landlords.

The Moplah rebellion was a turning point for Savarkar and Hindutva. In April 1920, the Khilafat movement took up the grievance of the Moplah tenants, where an unrest had been brewing over several years, even decades. The land tenure systems under the British Raj had placed unchecked powers in the hands of landlords. In the Malabar region, these powers were enjoyed by the upper-caste Hindu landlords, the Namboodri and Nair janmi, worsening the situation for tenants and cultivators, largely Muslim kanamdars and verupattam dars, who were locally called Moplahs. In his work on modern Indian history, historian Sumit Sarkar writes that an immediate consequence in Malabar was a 'strengthening of communal solidarity, with the number of mosques in Malabar going up from 637 in 1831 to 1058 by 1851, and with the Tangals of Mambram near Tirurangadi becoming increasingly prominent as the religious cum-political head of Moplah society.'[3]

People from the Cherumar castes, formerly untouchables, had converted to Islam, which promised equality and some degree of social mobility. 'Revolt became practically endemic,' writes Sarkar. Between 1836 and 1854, twenty-two tenant uprisings were recorded; more were added towards the end of the nineteenth century. Small bands of Moplahs attacked janmi properties and desecrated temples. They also courted death at the hands of police to die as shaheeds or martyrs. The roots of the revolt undoubtedly lay in agrarian distress. In Sarkar's estimation, Muslim and Hindu peasants suffered greatly under landlords. '...there was a 244% increase in rent suits and a 441% increase in eviction decrees between 1862 and 1880 in the talukas of south Malabar.'[4]

On 20 August 1921, an insurrection broke out when the police raided the Tirurangadi mosque in Malappuram district. Police stations were attacked, as were public offices and the residences of landlords. For several months, the British lost control of parts of Malabar; Khilafat 'republics' rose up instead under 'Presidents' Kunhammad Haji, Ali Musaliar and others. While the rebellion looked communal in appearance, it really was an anti-imperialist and anti-landlord agitation. Hindus, however, saw it as communal violence directed against them, a targeted ethnic cleansing. The revolt was violent; 600 Hindus were killed and around 2,500 were forced into conversion, according to Arya Samaj sources. These were small numbers, though, compared to the number of Moplah rebels who were affected—2,337 killed, 1,652 wounded and 45,404 taken prisoner. In a particularly horrific incident, known as the 'Black Hole' of Podanur, sixty-six Moplah rebels were asphyxiated to death in a wagon by imperial forces.

Despite the agrarian roots and anti-imperialist targets of the Moplah revolt, Hindu opinion sees this insurrection as a outright communal 'holocaust'. Over the decades, Moplah has acquired the same status of resentment for Hindus as the Kashmiri Pandit exodus from the Jammu and Kashmir Valley in the early 1990s. A hundred years after Khilafat and Moplah, Hindu discontent rekindled a version of this history and equated it to civil protests that erupted in 2019–2020. In historian K.N. Panikkar's analysis, in 1921, both Hindu and Muslim peasantry were equally exploited by the landed classes. 'Given the commonly shared economic discontent of the rural poor, both Hindus and Mappilas (or Moplahs), the social and ideological mediation of religion and culture formed the crucial element in peasant action,' he writes.[5] The Hindu peasants remained passive while the Mappila took a more militant approach. Why did the Hindu rural poor not revolt? Their ties with the upper-caste janmis were not just economic but also social and religious. For the Hindu peasant, the fear of social sanctions, caste censure, fines and excommunication was very real. They were inextricably tied to landlords via a system of exploitation that was sanctioned by religion. This religious organization did not provide ample avenues, particularly for the lower classes and castes, to congregate in common assemblies. The traditional intellectuals, as Panikkar calls them, were mostly associated with the landlord class in Hinduism.

Religion performed the opposite function for the Mappilas. Through a process of social and religious regeneration, they were able to redefine themselves in society. The Mappila traditional intellectuals—musaliars, mullas, qazis—did not have the same relationship with the landed classes as the Hindu intellectuals did. They saw the exploitation by landlords as a form of social injustice and preached that rising against this was a sureshot way to jannat or paradise. Killing a landlord who had evicted a tenant was not a sin but a meritorious act. At the local level, some factions of Mappilas associated the Khilafat movement with the establishment of an Islamic state. It seemed as if they responded more to the religious persuasion of Khilafat than to Gandhi's call for non-cooperation. While the prominent leaders of the Moplah rebellion—Ali Musaliar, Variyam Kunnath Kunhammad Haji (the subject of a 2020–21 Malayalam film), and Chembrasseri Thangal—were not involved in conversions, there were other local Mappila factions who carried out forced conversions and killings of those Hindus who refused to embrace Islam. It was also reported at the time that some members of this faction amused themselves by assigning Mappila names to women of Nair families, whom they would supposedly marry after conversion. Religion also played an important role in the assembly and organization of Mappilas; congregations took place and uprisings were planned in mosques. Perhaps the targeting of the Tirurangadi mosque in August 1921 by the police was deliberate.

There were long-term consequences to the Moplah rebellion. Society, particularly in Malabar, hardened along communal lines. For Savarkar, as mentioned before, the Moplah revolt was a major turning point in the history of Hindutva and the shaping of Hindutva masculinity. The Arya Samaj brought out its own version of what happened in Malabar (called 'Malabar Ka Hatyakand'), which included the indictment of Moplah leader Ali Musaliar and eyewitness accounts of their barbarity towards Hindu men and women. This was necessary reading for Savarkar, as well as inspiration for the fictional book he authored, loosely based on the events that took place in Malabar. In this work, as is the case with much of Savarkar's writing, there are elements that have come to define Hindutva masculinity—virulent hatred for the 'other' personified by the Muslim, an unwavering opposition to non-violence and a stance on caste to serve Hindu unity, which bears little resemblance to anti-caste movements for equality.

Like Panikkar observed, the Mappila Muslims were organized and motivated by religion with the promise of martyrdom and paradise, unlike the Hindus, whom the caste divisions within their religion had made weaker. Savarkar's fictionalized account is mostly the story of a small fanatical faction in Malabar that carried out forced conversions and killings. In graphic detail, he writes about a Mappila who boasts of having killed all the Hindus residing in a taluk in the Malabar region, sparing only those who converted to Islam; who had destroyed all the temple idols and taken the lives of unborn Hindu children. According to him, an Islamic Khilafat republic would be established; the violence, or jihad, of the Mappila would be rewarded with a place in jannat. In Hindutva's understanding, jihad means violence, destruction of property and the abduction of women. Jannat was described even more fancifully in the book, a place where rivers of alcohol and milk would flow freely; pomegranate and fig trees would be plentiful; each Muslim man would be surrounded by seventy beautiful virgins and boys for their pleasure; and a hundred-fold increase in their manliness.

The preface to the book sets the context. It asks the reader to imagine Aryavarta, the nation between the two Sindhus, as an ancient, shade-giving banyan tree. This wise tree is rotting; the termites of untouchability, child marriage, caste system and non-Vedic religions have chipped away at the roots. The result of this is that the storm of Islam from Arabia felled the tree of Aryavarta with great ease. Hindutva ideologues like Savarkar have particularly held untouchability and idol worship as responsible for the weakening of the Hindu in the face of constant threats.

In order to explain what happened in Malabar, Savarkar and Sampuranand examine caste relations in the region in some detail. According to them, the caste hierarchy of Malabar was arranged as follows: the Brahmin Namboodiri caste right at the top, the Kshatriya Nair caste below and castes like the Thiyyas, who were untouchables, out of the system altogether.

Untouchability was literally measured in terms of distance for the Namboodiris and Nairs—they were to keep a 24-feet distance from the Thiyyas, 36 feet from the Kanisans (or Kaniyars) and 72 feet from the Nayadis. They lamented that they did not distance themselves from mosquitoes, flies, dogs, cats, bees or wasps, but had strict rules on distancing between humans and humans. In his fictional account, Savarkar writes about a Brahmin by the name of Sthuleshwar Shastri, who refused to save Hindus against the onslaught of Muslim Mappilas, as his religion had been polluted by the lower castes who had entered his home, perhaps to seek refuge. So rigid were the rules of this oppressive system that Shastri refused to hand over his daughter to a Dalit's custody, who could have taken her to safety, preferring her to be abducted by the Mappila.

As mentioned earlier, Savarkar and Hindutva ideologues of the time had two preoccupations; the construction of the national identity or the Hindu, which depended on a hatred of the 'other'; and a unification of all Hindus, irrespective of caste, tribe and other such factors. They wrote with as much passion about caste as they did about an imagined enemy.

A nation, like other objects of ideology, is an imaginary cause, paradoxically produced by its effects. It only exists as long as its subjects believe in it, writes Slavoj Žižek. The national community is an imagined entity. Its substance is elusive, but very 'real'. It is ultimately undefinable and only manifestable through symbolic representation; in the case of Hindutva, they tried to achieve this via militarization.

Thomas Blom Hansen has argued that the basic impulse in any ideological cause, or for an imagined community, is the search for fullness. 'This search, in turn, constitutes the community, which only can exist as long as this fullness is not achieved. Once the fullness is achieved—and the "other" is eradicated—there can be no cause and hence no community.'[6]

What makes the Hindus a community at all?

The RSS ideologue M.S. Golwalkar refers to the Hindu as 'undefinable' and identifies the 'Hindu Nation' only as the feeling of being one while serving the nation. The coherence and unity of the Muslim community is, on the contrary, assumed without hesitation and exaggerated as 'excessive enjoyment'. The search for fullness, the overcoming of the 'lack' of being a full community, constitutes the national cause to Golwalkar. It is precisely the 'service to the motherland', the 'making of the nation' the recuperation of the not yet full-fledged national spirit, which makes the Hindus a community at all.[7]

3

Hindu Khatre Mein Hai

THE idea of '*Hindu khatre mein hai*' perhaps finds its origin in an essay called 'Is [the] Hindu a dying race?', authored by Colonel U.N. Mukherji as a series of articles for the daily newspaper *Bengalee*. The arguments made in this 1912 essay are extremely similar to those that appeared later in Savarkar's account of the Moplah revolt—the comparison between Hindu and Muslim organization, population and unity. In a way, the essay also serves as Mukherji's rumination on the condition of Hindus in Bengal at the turn of the twentieth century, which he said was characterized by widespread poverty.[1] Mukherji was widely credited as the man who directed the Hindu intelligentsia's attention towards the (apparently) declining Hindu population in Bengal as a precursor of things to come.

Colonel Mukherji painted a grim picture for Hindus in the Bengal province between the censuses from 1872 to 1901. He argued that over the span of three decades, the Muslims in Bengal, who were a minority, became nearly 25 lakh more in number than Hindus; their population increased by more than 33 per cent whereas the Hindus only grew by 17 per cent. Mukherji anxiously reported that calculations were on at the census office to calculate the number of years it would take for Hindus to disappear altogether from Bengal.[2] His dire warnings have not come true, nor are they likely to. The Muslim population in the country is less than 15 per cent of the total population. But despite the irrelevance of his analysis, his book is still in print—one edition carries a glowing introduction by RSS ideologue and Member of Parliament Rakesh Sinha, who has said that Mukherji's writings 'had the most formidable impact on the Hindu psyche.'[3] He might be right. Fake news about an exploding Muslim population can still go viral in India, with many believing it to be entirely possible.[4]

The false alarm having gone off, Mukherji built on this hypothesis by arguing that Hindus were diminishing because of conversions and the practice of polygamy and widow remarriage among Muslims.[5]

Perhaps the first mention of 'love jihad' can be found in this essay. Out of forty cases of conversion from Hindu to Muslim in the 24 Parganas district, he reported, twenty-two were for 'love'. In Dacca (now Dhaka), nine out of fourteen conversions were for 'love'.[6] One can almost picture Colonel Mukherji, who was a doctor by profession, sitting in a dispensary attending to 'Hindu carpenters and Muslim duftries', churning out observations that had no credible sources, only dire warnings for the Hindu race. He further propagated the theory of the dying Hindu race by claiming that poor Hindus had lost trades and jobs to stronger, healthier and more numerous Muslims. Why is it, he asked, that Hindus have disappeared from trades and occupations such as cooks, boatmen, sailors, machine-room workers, masons and carpenters? 'By 30,' he wrote from his observation deck at his dispensary, 'the Hindu mechanic is a physical wreck, broken down by disease and drink as a consequence of scanty food and an ill-regulated life.' In his estimation, the Hindus in Bengal were poorer, disunited and more disease-prone in comparison with the Muslims.[7] In what will become a familiar Hindutva argument, Mukherji also attacked the caste system among Hindus, blaming it for their lack of social mobility and prosperity.

The so-called high castes who form less than 13 per cent of the total number of Hindus regard any association such as sitting together with 30 per cent of the co-religionists as degrading and with the majority 57 per cent of the remaining Hindus as contaminating. Any water touched by 57 out of 100 Hindus will be regarded as polluted by the remaining 43.[8] [sic]

As devastating as this critique was (and is), the notion behind it had nothing to do with egalitarianism. The motive was to emphasize that the only answer to Muslim fundamentalism and assertion in Hindustan is Hindu unity.

Nearly a decade before the Moplah rebellion, Mukherji wrote about the religious organization and training of Muslims. According to him, all year round, without ostentation or question, Muslims gather at mosques, worship together and receive some form of moral training from muezzins and ulemas. As described in the previous chapter, this happened in Malabar—mosques became sites of moral and political revival of the oppressed classes against the oppressors. Hindus, disorganized and disunited, believed in practising untouchability more than brotherhood. This is another powerful myth that has been reproduced by Hindu nationalist discourse—Muslims are organized, secretive and embody their religion fanatically. Mahatma Gandhi had a moral philosophy built on the pillars of truth and non-violence, but this moral revolution was rejected by Hindutva ideologues.

One of Savarkar's specific critiques of Gandhi was that Hindus had been weakened after adopting his teaching of non-violence, 'precisely at a historical juncture when Hindu militarization in the face of the Muslim threat was imperative'. Muslims, Savarkar says, didn't care for Gandhi's non-violence and, therefore, had gained superiority in the army and the armed police, while 'the martial instinct of Hindus has been diluted by the adoption of non-violence'. Savarkar condemned the doctrine of absolute non-violence; instead, he said that the Hindu Mahasabha accepted the 'virtue of relative non-violence'. In 1942, at the twenty-fourth session of the Mahasabha, Savarkar noted that 'because of the Gandhian claim that the true spiritual warrior was the spinner of homemade cloth, Hindus had largely refused to join the Army, so that the percentage of Muslims in the Army had risen to 62 per cent.'[9] It was only after the Sabha generated military enthusiasm among Hindus that thousands of them joined the forces, bringing the Muslim representation down to 32 per cent.

The Hindu nationalist discourse, then and now, imagines an invading Muslim enemy pitted against a weakened Hindu. In medieval India, Hindus, weakened by non-violence, feared invasions by iconoclastic Muslim invaders. In pre-independent India, Hindus, represented by Mahasabhaites, were ruled by the fear that they were a dying race and angered by Mahatma Gandhi and the Indian National Congress's policies of Muslim appeasement in the guise of Hindu–Muslim unity. Hindutva proponents like Godse found the addition of '*Eshwar Allah tero naam*' to Gandhi's favourite bhajan, '*Raghupati Raghav Raja Ram*', abhorrent. They protested and demonstrated against the reading of the Quran at Gandhi's prayer meetings. They utterly resented the fact that (in their interpretation) Gandhi did not say a word against the atrocities against Hindus in Noakhali but went on his last satyagraha for the release of 55 crore rupees to Pakistan and for the celebration of the Urs at the dargah of Qutbuddin Bakhtiar Kaki in Delhi. The Hindu Mahasabha, including Nathuram Godse, Narayan Apte, Gopal Godse, Madanlal Pahwa, Vishnu Karkare, Digambar Badge and Vinayak Damodar Savarkar, hated that an old fakir could hold their ancient nation to ransom as per his idiosyncratic whims. It is not surprising that many of these apprehensions continue to haunt contemporary Indian society and shape Hindu masculinity.

✻

How does Hindutva perceive Hindu masculinity? Conversely, how does Hindutva perceive Muslim masculinity and why is it a threat?

From the Moplah episode, Hindutva ideologues deduced that Hindus were threatened by Muslim Mappilas, who were better organized on religious lines and predisposed towards action, even violence. The divided Hindu was weak, ineffectual and offered little retaliation. This assessment of the 'weak Hindu male' stretches in time, from the first Islamic invasions of Mahmud Ghazni and Moplah to an imagined attack in the twenty-first century. A particularly insightful argument by Hansen observes that 'recuperation of masculinity, the overcoming of emasculation, lies at the heart of the quest for national strength and national self-confidence which has been a persistent theme in Hindu nationalist movements in India for a century.' Could this explain why the idea of '*Hindu khatre mein hai*' finds relevance even today?

In the writings of Hindutva ideologues, a preconceived idea of the Muslim exists, which forms the basis for defining Hindu masculinity. Hansen argues that their construction of the Muslim identity is 'not just effects of momentous "poisoning" of the people by manipulators or criminals. They are widely existing forms of subjectivity, based on widely disseminated "mythical knowledge of the Other"'. Hindutva has aggregated everyday suspicions and misrecognitions between Hindus and Muslims and created powerful myths about the 'other' that are reproduced in the nationalist discourse. Why does the Hindu find himself in danger ever so often; why does the Hindu still believe in the possibility of an Islamic invasion or an Islamic state through proselytization (hence the belief in love jihad and in the need for ghar wapsi); why is the Muslim the foremost anti-national in the Hindu conception (hence the NRC and CAA)? These are powerful myths that animate the nationalist discourse even today, the seeds of which were sown by Vinayak Damodar Savarkar when he defined the essentials of Hindutva and who is a Hindu.

The Hindutva view of Hindu masculinity is also in relation to the 'other'—another myth-making process. Despite calling India their motherland and fatherland, the Muslims have failed to assimilate the Indian spirit. The Muslim is essentially expansive, aggressive, intolerant and poses a threat to Indian culture. Hindutva ideologues write that 'Muslims will always have a capacity and propensity for violence, secrecy and dominance ... its very existence prevents the enjoyment of Hindu nationality as it "steals the national enjoyment", weakening Hindu nation-ness by the fear, envy, and 'perverse attraction' it engenders.'[10] There are grim lessons for the Hindu who does not take this seriously, they warn. In the ideological struggle for Hindustan (in their world view), Islamic fundamentalism must be met with Hindu unity, which continues to be elusive.

Among the intelligence files of the Gandhi murder case is a copy of an alleged pamphlet (undated) belonging to the Calcutta Muslim League that was secretly obtained by Hindus. The contents of this pamphlet are reproduced below in full to illuminate the myth-making process.

All the Muslim Leaguers must obey these instructions and put into action.

Pakistan Zindabad. Qaid-i-Azam Zindabad.

1. All members of Islam shall die for Pakistan.
2. With Pakistan established the whole India should be conquered.
3. All the Muslims should join hand in this sacred work of Islam.
4. One Muslim gets the right of five Hindus, i.e. for the murder of one Muslim five Hindus must be murdered.
5. Until Pakistan Empire is established in India the following steps should be taken by all League Muslims.
6. All the Muslim Kingdoms should join hands in the sacred work of Islam.
7. All factories and shops owned by the Hindus should be burnt, destroyed and looted and the loot must be given to the League Officers.
b. All Muslim Leaguers should carry weapons with them for their defence and assault on Hindus.
c. All Nationalists Muslims, if they do not join the League, must be murdered by the secret League Gestapo.
d. Hindu must be murdered gradually and their population reduced.
e. All Hindu temples must be destroyed.
f. Congress newspaper offices should be destroyed by the League Gestapo.

g. Congress leaders must be murdered one by one at every moment by secret methods.

h. Karachi, Delhi, Bombay, Madras and Calcutta should be paralysed by December 1946 by Muslim League volunteers.

i. Muslims should carry on stabbing on the vast scale all over India and be prepared for the final [sic].

j. Muslim Leaguers must never be allowed to work in Army, Navy and other Government services or any Hindu firm.

k. Financial help is being given by the Nizam, Bhopal State and rich League Zamindars and Merchants.

l. Punjab, Singh, Bengal and other Muslim states will be the place of manufacturing of all kinds of weapons which will be distributed privately all over India by the Chief Leaguers to establish Pakistan in India.

m. All Muslims should carry weapons and at least pocketknives of all kinds.

n. Drive all Hindus from India. Destroy them.

o. All Muslims should carry transport. They should be well organised and used for battle against Hindus.

The provenance of this alleged pamphlet is unknown. However, it was translated and circulated among Hindus with the instruction that 'it is the duty of every Hindu that if he is a literate [sic] he should prepare four copies of this pamphlet and distribute them among Hindus; and if he is illiterate he should hear it'. The contents of this alleged Muslim League pamphlet, whose authenticity was never established, speaks to the fears the Hindu nationalists have harboured over centuries. It was their worst nightmare come true. The events that followed—a violent and irreversible partition—only confirmed the mutual suspicions of Hindus and Muslims and strengthened the mythmaking around their communal identities.

In the Hindu Mahasabha papers, there is a letter dated 18 December 1946 from Mrs Tatiana Shaha to Ashutosh Lahiri, the general secretary of All India Hindu Mahasabha and a close aide of Savarkar. Reading the letter, it would appear that the Mahasabha had succeeded in institutionalizing Savarkar's definition of who is a Hindu and the construction of nationalism by Hindu militarization.

Mrs Shaha writes in the letter,

We always felt that a strong and patriotic organization of only Hindus is destined to play quite a significant role in the liberation of this country, more over before such a menace as Communal Muslim League, with its provocative Policy, which led to so many disasters in the very recent past. The united Hindus are invincible power, while according to the late Pandit Madan Mohan Malyajee [sic], every plead of Hindus for reconciliation and every act of kindness and tolerance is interpreted by the other side as nothing but weekness[sic]. It is also universally known and recognized that a strong

Army or a Strong Organization is the basis of Peace and Progress.[11]

In a nutshell, this is the myth of Hindu masculinity that Hindutva wants us to believe: the passive, non-violence-loving Hindu man is an effeminate weakling who is unable to protect the Hindu society from attacks, especially from the violence of Muslims. The organized, fanatic Muslim is the threat that is blocking the fullest expression of proud Hindu manliness, really 'stealing the national enjoyment'. The Hindu man is not embodied by Gandhi—whose adherence to ahimsa has led to the mutilation of the land between the two Sindhus and the weakness of the Hindu race—but by Godse, who embodies the righteous valour of Shivaji, who does not hesitate to use violence for the protection of Hindus.

Just as the idea that the 'other' is Muslim is endlessly repeated by Hindu nationalist discourse, so are the myths of 'excessive desire of Muslims'—four wives, many children and the ease of triple talaq divorce. In the Hindu nationalist conception, Muslim manliness complements/fits in neatly with Hindu weakness. It does not matter if such Muslims exist in reality or not, the myth is woven around an abstract idea of a Muslim 'other'. How then does the Hindu male recover his masculinity? By an intense hatred of the 'other'. Hansen observes that the myth-making process cuts both ways among Hindus and Muslims; Muslim men have used the mythical knowledge reproduced in the nationalist discourse to assert their pride and masculinity. In this construction of Hindu masculinity, the Hindu male is incomplete without the Muslim; in fact, he is defined by what

173

he is not. Hindustan (or Bharat or even Aryavarta) is defined by the actions of the 'other'—the invading, proselytizing, violent Muslim stealing Hindu women, Hindu property and Hindu manhood.

There is no doubt that Gandhi rejected this overanxious Hindu masculinity. For him, Hindu–Muslim unity was an integral feature of the 'moral and political revival of India'. According to him, ahimsa or non-violence was not a passive stance of avoiding harm or violence, but was

...a positive state of love, of doing good even to the evildoer. But it does not mean helping the evil-doer to continue the wrong or tolerating it by passive acquiescence—on the contrary, love, the active state of ahimsa, requires you to resist the wrong-doer by disassociating yourself from him even though it may offend him or injure him physically.[12]

4

The Cult of Godse

ON 30 January 2021, the seventy-third death anniversary of Mahatma Gandhi, his murderer Nathuram Godse was the top trend on social media. In fact, this has been the case for the last few years. That a political assassin should attain some kind of notoriety is expected, but in contemporary India, Godse is eulogized, even celebrated, as a patriot of the same standing as Gandhi, Nehru or Patel. Members of Parliament express admiration for him without any misgivings.[1] His statues are being erected and worshipped; he trends as #GodseTumAmarRaho. The cult of Nathuram Godse, Ramachandra Guha writes, is no longer marginal, it has gone mainstream.[2] But there was always a cult.

Even in 1948, just days after he had assassinated Gandhi, Godse was seen as a 'jatiya gaurab'—a national hero—in some quarters. On 6 February 1948, an anonymous letter arrived from Bara Bazar, Calcutta, at the Tughlaq Road police station in Delhi, addressed to Nathuram Godse. Translated by the Criminal Investigation Department (CID), Delhi, from Hindi to English, the letter, which was recorded as a secret note of the intelligence department, read as follows:

> You GREAT PRIDE of Hindus,
>
> You have done a great service to the Hindu Community by murdering Gandhi who was a sympathiser of Muslims. You have, therefore, become immortal in the history of Hindu Community. God had given you birth to murder Gandhi which you have done. Now you should leave for paradise with a desire that God may send another soul like Siva Ji who may rescue the Hindu Community from Nehru, a slave of Muslims, and a slur on the name of Hindu Community, so that Hindu religion may shine all over the world.
>
> You may rest assured that Hindu Community will never forget you and will not rest till Nehru who is a blot on the whole Hindu Community is not done away with because of the fact that in the regime of Nehru Hindus are being perished in lacs in Pakistan. Nehru instead of protecting Hindus, is using his sword to crush the Hindu Community.
>
> May God Jawahar Lal Nehru finishes! [sic]

While this was an individual act bearing no name, reading the letter gives an inkling of the right wing's obsessive hatred towards Jawaharlal Nehru and his political dynasty, that continues to this day. The cult of Godse did not end here.

On 10 November 1948, Nathuram Godse read out a written statement in the court of Special Judge Atma Charan during the Red Fort trial. The statement was 126 pages long, consisting of five parts and five annexures. In these five parts, he subjected Mahatma Gandhi's politics to an X-ray examination, calling him an anti-national (and thereby coining and defining a term that has found contemporary relevance). His statement set out a detailed rationale for his treasonous act of murdering the father of a nation that had just won independence. Godse also took sole responsibility for the assassination, scoffing at the accusation of a Savarkar-led conspiracy and also eschewing any involvement with Madanlal Pahwa's failed attempt.

The Hindu Mahasabha made consistent efforts to rehabilitate Godse's image. In 1954, a few years after the ban on the Hindu Mahasabha and RSS was lifted, intelligence agencies recorded coordinated, clandestine endeavours by various people to publish and circulate Nathuram Godse's statement, 'Meri Kahani'. Efforts were on from Ambala to Dehradun to translate Godse's statement into English and print copies of it in both English and Hindi for circulation at the Hyderabad session of the All India Mahasabha. Members of the Ambala chapter of the Hindu Mahasabha, Professor Manohar Lal and Inder Sain, approached the Delhi chapter to publish the English edition of the statement, while Suresh Mohan Bhargav of the Hindu Rashtra Sena secured copies for surreptitious sale in Hyderabad. In Dehradun, Dr Satya Prakash was in charge of translating 'Meri Kahani' into English, while in Delhi,

Mahasabha worker Panna Lal made arrangements to send 150 Hindi and 1,000 English copies to Hyderabad for South Indian audiences. Reading Godse's statement, the Mahasabha realized, was essential.

Godse's trial began on 22 June 1948 after a five-month-long investigation by the police. The evidence amounted to 1,131 printed pages of foolscap size and a supplementary volume of 115 pages of cyclostyled foolscap paper. On 10 February 1949, the court pronounced its judgment—Nathuram Godse and Narayan Apte were sentenced to death and the remaining five to imprisonment for life. The convicted were given fifteen days to file appeals; in four days' time, appeals were filed in the Panjab High Court on behalf of all seven convicted persons. Godse did not challenge his conviction on the charge of murder, nor did he question the death sentence. What he challenged was the finding that there was a conspiracy. Perhaps he did so in order to protect his father figure, Savarkar.

Justice G.D. Khosla has described the proceedings in the Panjab High Court in his book *The Murder of the Mahatma: and Other Cases from a Judge's Notebook*. The Panjab High Court was, at the time, located in Simla. The court convened in the summer residence of the Viceroy, the Peterhoff. He wrote:

The hearing began on May 2, 1949. It was a bright day with the gold of the sun lying in a thin layer on the lawns of Peterhoff. There was a cold breath in the air, and the ball-room was warmed by a dozen or so electric fires. Policemen stood guard at the entrance, and admission to the courtroom was regulated by passes.

The room was full to capacity. Godse had refused to be represented by a lawyer, and had pleaded poverty in order to be permitted to appear in person and argue his appeal. The plea was granted. His small defiant figure with flashing eyes and close-cropped hair offered a remarkable, immediately noticeable contrast to the long row of placid and prosperous-looking lawyers who represented his accomplices, Khosla wrote. According to the judge, Godse's plea of poverty was an excuse. The real reason behind his wanting to be present was a desire to show himself as a fearless patriot and an ardent advocate of Hindu ideology.

Khosla continued:

> The highlight of the appeal before us was the discourse delivered by Nathuram Godse in his defence. His main theme was the nature of a righteous man's duty, his dharma as laid down in the Hindu scriptures. He made moving references to historical events and delivered an impassioned appeal to Hindus to hold and preserve their motherland and fight for it with their very lives. He ended his peroration on a high note of emotion, reciting verses from Bhagwadgita.[3]

The audience, Khosla wrote, was moved. The room fell silent, with some people in tears, others pretending to hide their tears. Justice Khosla felt as if he were in a scene from a melodrama. Even as he pointed out the irrelevance of what Godse was saying, the audience listened to the murderer, transfixed. To them, Godse's performance was the only worthwhile part of the court proceedings. 'I have no doubt,' Khosla wrote, 'that had the audience of that day been constituted into a jury and entrusted with the task of deciding Godse's appeal, they would have brought in a verdict of Not Guilty by an overwhelming majority.'[4]

In contemporary India, the image of Nathuram Godse is undergoing rehabilitation once again. The act of killing Mahatma Gandhi is no longer seen as treasonous; in fact, Godse today is the epitome of patriotism. He is the ideal Hindu—one whose sacrifice matches Mahatma Gandhi's, one who has followed in the steps of Shivaji and one who is a committed ideologue like Savarkar. India's past, present and future, one could argue, is now a contestation of two interpretations of our history—Gandhi's secular Hinduism (*sarva dharma sama bhava*) versus Savarkar's hardline Hindutva (*akhanda Bharat amar rahe*). Even Godse agreed that Gandhi and Savarkar's ideologies had 'contributed more to mould the thought and action of mother India during the last fifty years or so, than any other single factor had done.'[5]

The Original Anti-national

As Nathuram Godse assumes renewed relevance in today's India, contentious and perplexing questions have emerged about our history and where we go from here. How can both Mahatma Gandhi and his killer be national heroes or patriots of equal measure? Why was Gandhi called anti-national? The answers are complex, and some of them lie in Godse's own statement. In his deconstruction of the Father of the Nation,

Mahatma Gandhi was 'guilty of blunder after blunder, failure after failure and disaster after disaster'.[6]

In more than three decades of his political career, Gandhi could not claim a single political victory, Godse wrote. According to him, the Mahatma's political journey can be divided into three parts. The first part comprises the years between 1914 and 1939–40, when Mohandas Karamchand Gandhi returned to India and started propounding the slogans of truth and non-violence from the banks of the Sabarmati in Gujarat. Godse calls these maxims an ostentatious parade; they were lofty principles that were absolutely useless in day-to-day life. 'Gandhi was a violent pacifist, who brought untold calamities on the country in the name of truth and non-violence, while Rana Pratap, Shivaji and the Guru (Gobind) will remain enshrined in the hearts of their countrymen for ever and for ever [sic] for the freedom they brought to them.'[7]

Under Gandhi's watch, Godse claims that one-third of India—the boundaries of which he defined from Karachi to Assam, and from the North West Frontier Province to Cape Comorin—was partitioned. Under his stubborn leadership, more temples were desecrated than ever before, more forcible and fraudulent conversions happened and more women were outraged. Under the garb of Hindu–Muslim unity, Gandhi, Godse claimed, waged a pro-Muslim appeasement policy, from the miscalculated support to the Khilafat movement—which was followed by the bloody Moplah rebellion—to the Communal Award in 1932, which gave separate electorates to Muslims in British India.[8]

It has been documented earlier that India's independence from colonial power was not Mahatma Gandhi's sole preoccupation. He also promoted religious harmony between conflicting communities, the abolition of untouchability from Hinduism and establishing a home-grown economic model of development that centred on self-reliance, a term that has been appropriated by the present government. Gandhi's continuous quest for Hindu–Muslim unity rankled Godse, Savarkar and other Hindutvawadis to no end. In his statement, Godse devotes considerable space to attack Gandhi's pursuit and practice of secularism. Religious unity and harmony, the practice of truth and ahimsa—these were at the heart of Gandhi's actions, even at the bloodiest of times like in Noakhali in 1946 or Delhi in 1947. To Godse these principles were absurd, far removed from reality. For him, Gandhi's approach to Hindu–Muslim harmony was a one-way street—the Hindu concedes, the Muslim takes. All of the Mahatma's experiments, he wrote, were at the expense of Hindus. Godse explained what according to him was Gandhi's one-sided practice of secularism with point after point in his statement.

One of the points made by Godse is regarding the decision on the national language of India. 'By all tests of a scientific language, Hindi has the most prior claim to be accepted as the National language of the country,' he wrote. At first, he claims, Gandhi was enthusiastic about Hindi as the national language. But when he found out that Muslims were not too keen on the idea, Gandhi became a champion for the cause of Hindustani. Godse is scathing in his criticism of this U-turn: 'Everybody in India knows there is no language called Hindustani; it has no grammar; it has no vocabulary; it is a mere dialect; it is spoken but not written. It is a bastard tongue and a cross-breed between Hindi and Urdu and not even the Mahatma's sophistry could make it popular.'[9]

Godse claimed that 'Badshah Ram' and 'Begum Sita' came into use but Gandhi never dared to disrespect Muslims by prefacing Jinnah with 'Srijut' (the earlier form of Sri) or Maulana Azad with 'Pandit'. 'The barest common sense should make it clear to the meanest intelligence that the language of 80 per cent of the people must be the language of the country,' he wrote. For Godse, Gandhi was trying to smuggle in a foreign language—Urdu—under the garb of Hindustani and reject the pure language of the land, which was the only natural choice, all in the name of Hindu–Muslim unity.

If Godse argued for Hindi to be given the status of official language, Savarkar took this demand back a few centuries to make a case for Prakrit, 'the eldest daughter of Sanskrit'. Sanskrit was the language of pandits and princes, whereas Prakrit could be understood from Rameswaram to Haridwar, from rajasabhas to bazaars. Sanskrit must remain the 'cherished and sacred possession of our race, contributing powerfully to the fundamental unity of our people,' whereas Prakrit conveyed 'the living and throbbing thoughts of the people in all their freshness and vigour and precision'. For Savarkar, Prakrit was Hindi or Hindustani, 'the national language was but an outward expression of this inward unity of our national life'.

Godse argued in favour of 'Vande Mataram', the national song composed by Bankim Chandra Chatterjee, and 'Shiva Bavani', fifty-two verses on Maratha warrior Shivaji's exploits composed by the poet Bhushan. 'Vande Mataram' was replaced by Rabindranath Tagore's 'Jana Gana Mana' as the National Anthem after the 1937 Indian National Congress working committee meeting in Calcutta. The meeting was presided over by Jawaharlal Nehru who, after consultation with Tagore, decided that 'Vande Mataram' in its entirety was disrespectful of Muslim religious sentiment. The working committee passed a resolution to this effect. Bankim Chandra's song is an ode to worshipping Mother India; it equates the Hindu goddesses Durga and Lakshmi to the motherland. In Islam, the apotheosis of anyone but God is not acceptable. As a result of this, 'Vande Mataram' became India's national song, not anthem, of which only the first two stanzas are sung.

'Could anything be more demoralized or pitiful than this brazen-faced action against a song of worldwide fame? Gandhi's Hindu-Muslim Unity idea only meant, surrender, capitulate, and concede whatever the Muslims wanted,' Godse wrote. 'No wonder the Will o'the Wisp unity never came and never could have come.'[10]

The issue of 'Vande Mataram' continues to rear its head. The heir of Hindu nationalism, the BJP, has time and again whipped up anger and suspicion against those who have refused to sing 'Vande Mataram'. In 2019, Pratap Chandra Sarangi, an MP from Odisha who faces charges in the gruesome murder of Australian missionary Graham Staines, asked if those who refuse to utter 'Vande Mataram' have any right to live in the country. In the same year, Amit Shah said that refusing to sing the song amounted to treason. In 2018, Amit Shah delivered the first memorial lecture on Bankim Chandra Chatterjee in

Kolkata, where he blamed the Congress for leading India to partition by its incomplete acceptance of 'Vande Mataram'. 'For instance, the slogan Vande Mataram (I revere the Mother), which was the rallying cry of the nationalist struggles, could also become a divisive point during Hindu-Muslim riots.'[11]

In the same vein, Godse had claimed that Gandhi had banned the recital of Shiva Bavani because the refrain of the poem says, 'If there was no Shivaji, the entire country would have been converted to Islam.'

The second period of Gandhi's politics, Godse wrote and read out in court, was between 1939–40 and 3 June 1947, when the Mountbatten Plan was agreed upon and Pakistan came into existence, despite years of concessions on communal bases. The final period of Gandhi's politics, Godse says, was the period between Partition and the day of the final satyagraha, 13 January 1948, which resulted in the payment of 55 crore rupees to Pakistan. In Godse's retelling of Mahatma Gandhi's political journey, what stands out is the Father of the Nation's irresponsible pursuit of the phantom of Hindu–Muslim unity with the impossible-to-practice principles of truth and non-violence. In his eyes, Gandhi's stubborn adherence to ahimsa was an act of hubris that betrayed a 'total ignorance of the springs of human action'. The teachings of ahimsa, as advocated by Gandhi, 'would ultimately result in the emasculation of the Hindu Community incapable of resisting the aggression or inroads of other communities especially the Muslims'.

By the time undivided India was inching towards a blood-soaked independence, Godse wrote that he had 'lost all control over his feelings'. His emotional rhetoric notwithstanding,

Gandhi's murder investigation and subsequent commissions of inquiry left no doubt that the assassination was a planned conspiracy by members of a militant Hindu organization, not the violent reaction of an emotionally high-strung individual. 'Gandhiji,' Godse wrote, 'is being referred to as the father of the nation—an epithet of high reverence. But if so, he has failed in his paternal duty ... He has proved to be the father of Pakistan.'[12] He said that 'as a dutiful son of Mother India' he had to put an end to the life of the 'so-called' Father of the Nation who had brought on the vivisection of his motherland. And in the end, Nathuram Godse, the dutiful son, was sacrificing his life to save that of Vinayak Damodar Savarkar, his ideological parent.

Epilogue

8 August 2021

SEVENTY-FOUR years ago, the August conspiracy unfolded around this time, when V.D. Savarkar boarded a plane to Delhi along with Nathuram Godse and Narayan Apte. As we pieced together evidence, intelligence note by intelligence note, it became clear to us that the conspiracy to murder Mahatma Gandhi was not the handiwork of a lone wolf or a few fanatic members of the Hindu Mahasabha. Most importantly, it was not conceived just a few weeks before 30 January 1948. The new evidence we have presented in this book traces the origins of the conspiracy to a time as early as a week before

Independence Day in 1947. In our opinion, this discovery has enormous significance for the contemporary understanding of a defining moment in India's history.

First, it challenges the widely held perception that the assassination was a response to Mahatma Gandhi's insistence that the Government of India pay fifty-five crore rupees to Pakistan, and the rehabilitation of Muslims from December 1947 to January 1948. Even the Jeevan Lal Kapur Commission, which was set up two decades later to re-examine the assassination, focused only on the key events from December 1947 onwards.

Second, the evidence we have put forth—re-enacting the events from 8 August 1947 until the murder—serves as a time capsule of the political struggles that had been unfolding over four decades, in which Gandhi's politics of non-violence and Savarkar's programme of Hindutva feature prominently. Let us go back to Gandhian scholar K.P. Shankaran's question that is central to our book: *which* Gandhi was killed? To arrive at that answer, we need to dissect the why and ask all over again: *why* was Gandhi killed? In Nathuram Godse's statement before the trial court during the Gandhi murder trial, the following claim offers some clues: 'The problem of the State of Hyderabad which had been unnecessarily delayed and postponed has been rightly solved by our Government, by the use of armed force— after the demise of Gandhiji. The present Government of the remaining India is seen taking the course of practical politics.'

The 'solution' referred to here was the killing of 20,000– 47,000 ordinary Muslims by the state, according to *Destruction of Hyderabad* by noted lawyer and political commentator A.G.

Noorani, who accessed the Sunder Lal Committee report on the massacre of Hyderabad's Muslim population that was kept classified until 2013. In Godse's statement, he claimed that *he* had removed an obstacle for the newly born state.[1] It is important to remember that he says that with Gandhi gone, the government could follow 'practical politics', which in other words meant that the state was free to take violent recourse in the 'national interest'. According to Godse, he had killed a man who was anti-state and hence anti-national.

The unified Indian state that Godse, Savarkar and the Hindu right wing at large envisaged was promoted by the Hindu Mahasabha representation to the Cabinet Mission Delegation that came to India in 1946 to discuss the transfer of power from the British government to the Indian leadership. Their idea of the state was a strong federal government. In the 15 April 1946 representation, the Mahasabha (refer to point no. 4) stated: '[The] Indian constitution should be of a federal type with the Indian Union at the Centre and the Provinces and the Indian States as its federating units. The Constitution should leave no room for any province or an Indian state not to accede to the said Union or to secede therefrom.'

This conception of a strong centre, i.e., a strong federal government, and its implications, are explained further in point no. 5 of this representation:

The Constitution should provide for the grant of the utmost possible measure of autonomy to the federating units, but with the residue of powers vested in the centre. The Union government should have the power of superintendence and control in cases where the federating Units go wrong in respect of national policy or interest and should be strong enough to exercise this power effectively.

The state that Godse and the Hindu right wing was obsessed with was an aggressively centralized one, a type of state that Gandhi did not want because he envisioned the decentralization of power. Gandhi never wavered in his belief in and commitment towards non-violence and remained opposed to a monocentric state with brute machinery.

This begs the question: what kind of state did Gandhi envision? The first time he reflected upon the concept of the state was in 1909 in *Hind Swaraj or Indian Home Rule*. According to him, the state would be run by a Parliament chosen by the people, with power over finance, the police and other government machineries.[2] Gandhi's idea of the state subsequently went through at least two iterations. In 1931, Gandhi called for 'Purna Swaraj' or complete independence. The last iteration was developed a few months before his assassination in November 1947, when he called for Surajya or the good state, which he hoped the Indian state would embody. Our specific intention here is to dispel any doubt in the minds of readers that Gandhi was a violent anarchist or a utopian dreamer. He *did* believe in the institution of the state. But his state would be radically different from one that autocratically exercised top-down control over individuals. Like many other topics that he devoted his attention to, he had given considerable thought also to the idea of the state. The underlying nature of the state he wanted was a deeply ethical one, embodying Ram Rajya, just like the ethical religion he envisaged. Crucially, the Ram that Gandhi referred to was not the Hindu god; rather it was the ideal of an ethical state, where people were treated equally and the state was ruled according to the wishes of people.

In *Hind Swaraj*, Gandhi coined an aphorism that became popular—'English rule without Englishmen'. The context in which Gandhi wrote this is important to note. He was critiquing those elements of the freedom movement who wanted the independent India of the future to become just like Great Britain or Japan. These states were aggressively belligerent machines founded on territorial expansionism and ethnic nationalism. In Gandhi's *Surajya*, his last iteration that he composed before his assassination, his opposition to an aggressive state emanated from the fact that such states tend to be hegemonic and their totalitarian tendencies eventually oppressed citizens. He believed that in the name of doing good and promoting the national interest, such a state would eventually become repressive. In *Surajya*, the state is fair and equal towards every citizen. India is a multicultural and multi-religious society, therefore Gandhi's nationalism was non-aggressive and inclusive. So Surajya is, by default, a secular entity. Unlike his disciple Nehru, Gandhi did not look towards the West for his model of secularism. A deeply religious man who was at the same time opposed to religious or cultural nationalism of the type that Savarkar and the Hindu right generally wanted, Gandhi found the templates of his secularism within the Bhagavad Gita.

Gandhi's state derived its legitimacy from moral authority, while his critics' concept derived its legitimacy from the powers of the state. Gandhi defeated an illegitimate state through his non-violent protest of satyagraha, defying the powers that be when they did not act ethically. In the state that he envisaged, he provided an option for citizens to express their moral convictions through non-violent means. His ethical, non-aggressive state would respond compassionately, seeking a balance.

How would have Gandhi responded to the Hyderabad situation? Again, Godse provided a fair assessment in his detailed statement to the court.

Laik Ali the Prime Minister of Hyderabad had an interview with Gandhiji during the last week of January 1948. It was evident from the manner in which Gandhiji looked at these Hyderabad affairs, that Gandhiji would soon start his experiments of non-violence in the State of Hyderabad and treat Kasim Rizvi as his adopted son just as Suhrawardy. It was not at all difficult to see that it was impossible for the Government inspite of all the powers to take any strong measures against the Muslim State like Hyderabad so long as Gandhiji was there. Had the government then decided to take any military or police action against Hyderabad it would have been compelled to withdraw its decision just as was done in the case of the payment of Rs 55 crores, for Gandhiji would have gone on fast unto death and

Government's hands would have been forced to save the life of Gandhiji.[3] [sic]

It is difficult to disagree with Godse's account. If we apply the Surajya principle, Gandhi would have asked the state to respond to its citizens in a non-aggressive manner. This raises a fundamental question: was Gandhi such a pacifist that even in the face of imminent aggression he would not use violence for self-preservation? Ironically, Godse himself answers this question in a different part of his statement during the murder trial. Obviously, he did not intend to compliment Gandhi's political pragmatism. Instead, he pointed towards what he perceived as deep contradictions in Gandhian politics.

Godse based his argument on the support Gandhi extended to military action in Kashmir in late 1947.

A recent example of the inconsistency of his doctrine of non-violence is worth being noted in particular. The problem of Kashmir followed very closely that of Pakistan. Pakistan had begun a dreadful invasion to conquer and gulp down the Kashmir. H.H. the Maharaja of Kashmir had asked for help from the Nehru Government and the latter in return agreed to do so on the condition that Sheikh Abdullah would be made the Chief Administrator. On every important matter Pt. Nehru had consulted Gandhiji. There was every chance of partiality being done—Kashmir being the birthplace of Pt. Nehru. And to give no way to this partiality, Pt.

Nehru consulted Gandhiji about sending Military help to Kashmir and it was only on the consent of Gandhiji that Pt. Nehru sent troops for the protection and defence of Kashmir. Pt. Nehru has told this in one of his speeches. Our political leaders knew from the very beginning that the invasion of Kashmir by the raiders was supported by Pakistan. And it was, therefore, evident that sending help to the Kashmir meant waging war indirectly against Pakistan. Gandhiji himself was opposed to the war with arms, and he has told this to the entire world again and again. But he gave his consent to Pt. Nehru to send army in Kashmir. The only conclusion that could be drawn from what is happening in Kashmir is that, today after the attainment of freedom for the partitioned India, that under Gandhiji's blessings, our Government has resorted to the war where man-killing machinery is being used. Had Gandhiji been a firm belief in the doctrine of non-violence, he should have made a suggestion for sending Satyagrahis instead of the armed troops and tried the experiment. Orders should have been issued to send 'takalis' [hand spindles...] in place of rifles and 'Spinning-wheels' [charkhas] instead of the guns. It was a golden opportunity for Gandhiji to show the power of his Satyagraha by following his precept as an experiment at the beginning of our freedom.[4] [sic]

Here, Godse and Gandhi's critics were trying to present the Mahatma's ethical realism as a separate entity from his political realism. On the contrary, Gandhi was trying to strive for a delicate balance between the two. In simple terms, neither is violence the first response nor is it the last resort. For Gandhi, building a non-violent social order was his default response because that is the only permanent solution. However, in the interim, he was not categorically opposed to the legitimate use of state violence against domestic or external aggressions as a means of self-defence. So, Gandhi's support for the employment of the army in Kashmir can be understood in the context of his realistic assessment of the necessity and the limitations of the application of state violence.

Anthony Parel, while addressing the vexed theme of Gandhi and the state, develops an argument which supports our own understanding of Gandhi and the use of violence in self-defence.

Gandhi's weightiest contribution in support of the state's right to self-defence by military means came in his speech at the second Round Table Conference in London (1931). This was an official conference on a future constitution for India—the only such conference he ever attended. The significance of his statement therefore may not be underestimated. 'I think that a nation that has no control over her own defence forces and over her external policy is hardly a responsible nation. Defence, its Army, is to a nation the very essence of its existence, and if a nation's defence is controlled by an outside agency, no matter how friendly it is, then that nation is certainly not responsibly governed ... Hence I am here very respectfully to claim complete control over the Army, over the Defence forces and over

External Affairs ... I would wait till eternity if I cannot get control over Defence. I refuse to deceive myself that I am going to embark upon responsible government although I cannot control my defence. That is my fundamental position.'[5]

Gandhi's moral idealism, informed by political realism, hoped for a world order without war.

Godse thought he had killed a man who was anti-state and, hence, anti-national. But the difference between Gandhi and Godse (read, the Hindu right) can be properly understood through a basic disagreement over the morality of the use of aggression by the state. This was the key difference between the state as envisaged by Gandhi and the one conceptualized by everyone else, including his disciple Jawaharlal Nehru. Recall the poet Madhusoodanan Nair's lines mentioned in the Prologue—one Gandhi is he who walks alone on a path so difficult that even his followers (anugami) fail to accompany him.

Part Two

At the risk of repeating ourselves, we return to Nair's powerful question: Who is Gandhi? The one who sparked love and admiration in millions? The one who willingly sacrificed his frail body for satyagraha? Or the one who was able to tame the wildest among us and bring us together?

In Book 2, Chapter 3, we mentioned the letter that B.S. Moonje, the architect of the Hindu militarization project, penned to Sardar Vallabhbhai Patel in which he said, '...But after all is retaliation a crime?... retaliation is human nature and no moral crime.'[6] The provocation for the letter was that Moonje felt the 'sting' of Mahatma Gandhi's charge against Hindu aggressors, when he said that they were a disgrace to humanity.

Perhaps Moonje's frustration partly stemmed from the failure of his own ambitious Hindu militarization project. Even when faced with deadly forms of violence, there were no pan-India formations of a militant Hindu identity. All the ingredients for generating such a militarized formation were present at the time—a resurgent *'Hindu khatre mein hain'* narrative, thousands of potential recruits like Madanlal Pahwa who were victims of Partition violence, a Congress organization where the Gandhian influence had already begun to diminish and a few fully developed Hindu right-wing organizations. If Moonje's two-decade-long mobilization and propaganda towards the Hindu militarization project failed to take off during the 1946–48 period of intense and unprecedented violence, it must have gradually dawned on him that this project might never succeed.

This is not to say that there was no militant Hindu mobilization as a response to the violence supported by Muhammad Ali Jinnah's Muslim League or, at times, as retaliation and revenge for it. The failure that we are referring to here is the inability of the Hindu right-wing organizations to exploit a situation for which they had been preparing for many years. The rationale of Hindu militarization was partly a critique of Gandhian non-violence. Its proponents never ceased to believe that in the context of real-world violence, such as the

Moplah riots of 1921, the Gandhian methods of non-violence would inevitably fail. Were the Hindus genuinely concerned about being rendered defenceless, powerless and emasculated in front of a brute, well-organized violent machine? They certainly thought so.

Was this anxiety a reason for assassinating Gandhi? Consider the evidence carefully. Gandhi, the frail fakir, succeeded remarkably where militarization had failed. In Noakhali, in Bihar and subsequently in Delhi, Gandhi, through his practice of ahimsa, managed to restore peace to towns and cities ravaged by violence, hatred and suspicion. Noakhali, in particular, was a setback to people like Godse because they were convinced that while Hindus were willing to follow Gandhi in his path of non-violence, Muslims would never do so. However, in four months, Gandhi painstakingly convinced Muslim rioters, as well as Huseyn Shaheed Suhrawardy, the premier of Bengal who was accused of being responsible for the large-scale violence, to work towards a return to normalcy. This was a remarkable triumph over his critics. Despite this, Godse in his statement said that for many like him, the Gandhian resistance through non-violence was the biggest stumbling block to practical solutions. So what if nearly 50,000 lives had to be sacrificed in Hyderabad in the cause of national interest?

Gandhi's methods were deeply rooted in spiritualism, derived from the Bhagavad Gita. He was as much a political thinker as a social reformer. He made significant contributions to reforming Hindu religion by developing a radical interpretation of the Gita. His reforms were concentrated on infusing

Hindu religiosity with an ethical spirit, which would inform the foundations of India's polity. The book *Bhagavad Gita, According to Gandhi* is a very useful guide to understanding how he understood religion. On contentious topics such as cow slaughter, secularism and caste discrimination, the following interpretation was repeatedly emphasized by him:

> The men of self-realization look with an equal eye on a *brahmana* possessed of learning and humility, a cow, an elephant, a dog and even a dog-eater.
>
> That is to say, they serve every one of them alike, according to the needs of each. Treating a *brahmana* and *shwapaka* (dog-eater) alike means that the wise man will suck the poison off a snake-bitten *shwapaka* with as much eagerness and readiness as he would from a snake-bitten *brahmana*.[7]

Shankaran, in an opinion piece in *The Indian Express*, has argued:

> Gandhi's reading of the Gita, the most important text of the Vaishnava sect of Hinduism, is part of his internal criticism of popular Hinduism. He identified himself as a Hindu because of his birth and attempted to bring to it an ethical foundation in the place of pre-existing folk-based metaphysical themes—a project first initiated by the Buddha of the Nikayas. Gandhi thought, rightly or wrongly, that the Buddha was a great Hindu reformer.[8]

Gandhi reconfigured traditional Hindu religious vocabulary and offered his own radical interpretation of the Gita and Hinduism towards the non-aggressive nationalism that he tried to build. This project struck at the very heart of Hindutva.

Part Three

This brings us to the main point. Why is this topic relevant? Why does, and indeed why should Gandhi's assassination matter to us today?

We answer this question with a counterfactual scenario: if Gandhi had lived on, what would have happened?

The last major conceptual work by Gandhi was *Constructive Programme*, published in 1941. In our estimate, Gandhi has not yet received sufficient recognition as an economic thinker. In the post-war era, Gandhian imaginations of the polity and the independent Indian state were situated within a world stage of two conflicting economic ideologies, namely, communism and capitalism. From a Gandhian perspective, both these ideologies had a common structural flaw—inherent violence.

Chapter 13 of *Constructive Programme*, titled 'Economic Equality', highlights Gandhi's economic thought and his politics.

The opening two sentences are revealing: 'This last is the master key to non-violent Independence. Working for economic equality means abolishing the eternal conflict between capital and labour.'[9]

The same chapter explains his rationale and manifesto for attaining economic equality.

> It means the levelling down of the few rich in whose hands is concentrated the bulk of the nation's wealth on the one hand, and the levelling up of the semi-starved naked millions on the other. A non-violent system of Government is clearly an impossibility so long as the wide gulf between the rich and the hungry millions persists.[10]

Gandhi's manifesto for achieving economic equality goes on to declare:

> The contrast between the palaces of New Delhi and the miserable hovels of the poor labouring class nearby cannot last one day in a free India in which the poor will enjoy the same power as the richest in the land. A violent and bloody revolution is a certainty one day unless there is a voluntary abdication of riches and the power that riches give and sharing them for the common good. I adhere to my doctrine of trusteeship in spite of the ridicule that has been poured upon it. It is true that it is difficult to reach. So is non-violence.[11]

Today, philanthropy is a catchword in the uber-rich circles. Most of these philanthropic activities are structured through trusts, which are controlled by business families or their trusted employees. In a way, contemporary philanthropy generally operates through a trusteeship model, in an intriguing development of Gandhi's vision.

However, the form of trusteeship that Gandhi promoted was radically different because it was democratic in spirit and substance. This is clear from his critique of the princely states where he argued that their defenders were merely acting as custodians of public wealth. Gandhi's trusteeship model was opposed to elite formation. He was acutely aware of the princely clique of elites that had become an integral part of the Congress and he would have started his advancement of economic equality with them.

The remaining part of Chapter 13 of *Constructive Programme* touches upon this vital theme:

A society or a nation constructed non-violently must be able to withstand attack upon its structure from without or within. We have moneyed Congressmen in the organization. They have to lead the way. This fight provides an opportunity for the closest heart-searching on the part of every individual Congressman. If ever we are to achieve equality, the foundation has to be laid now. Those who think that the major reforms will come after the advent of Swaraj are deceiving themselves as to the elementary working of non-violent Swaraj. It will not drop from heaven all of a sudden one fine morning. But it has to be built up brick by brick by corporate self-effort.[12]

In our estimate, India and the world missed out on an economic model that would have been different from capitalism, socialism or communism, with their inherent forms of violence. A model that would be founded on non-violence, sustainability and inclusivity.

In post-independence India, and in the absence of Gandhi, the formation of the elite classes was sustained within the Congress to an extent. Many members of royal families as well as the bureaucrats who worked for them joined the Congress. This was followed by a steady flow of royalty, businessmen and others from the affluent classes who systematically attempted to appropriate the Congress in order to try and pursue their class-based interests. It is only to be expected that these elite groups looked after each other.[13]

If only Gandhi had lived long enough, we may have seen the fruits of a Gandhian solution to socioeconomic equality. That possibility can be seen in the 'bloodless revolution' of Bhoodan. In April 1951, the Gandhian satyagrahi Vinoba Bhave started the Bhoodan (land gift) movement in the village of Pochampalli in present-day Telangana. Of the 700 families in the village, two-thirds were landless and most of them were Dalits. Bhave convinced a local landlord to give away land to the landless. In six years, nearly two million hectares of land were received. The Bhoodan movement turned into the Bhoodan Act and the government oversaw distributing/redistributing land from the land bank. The movement later transformed into the Gramdan or village gift movement, in which 75 per cent of a village's residents once donated land for equal redistribution among all its residents.[14] This movement petered out by the 1970s and the state, as the custodian of the land bank, failed to redistribute all the land that had been gifted away. The Bhoodan movement also saw some short-lived offshoots, such as sampatti-dan (wealth gift), shramdan (labour gift) and sadhandan (gift of implements for agricultural operations). Bhoodan was a radical solution to the problem of inequality. Only Gandhi himself or a true Gandhian could have conceived this idea and turned it into a mass movement by urging people to think actively of the welfare of the underprivileged.

In other words, the Gandhian character of nationalism, predicated on the unwavering pursuit of ethics and social welfare through satya and ahimsa, lived on for a while through the Bhoodan movement. It reflected the Gandhian vision of a non-coercive, non-violent state. This was in complete contrast to the anxiously antagonistic character of nationalism that Savarkar had bequeathed to Hindus, the mentality of cosa nostra powered by a sense of opposition to the other.

Thomas Blom Hansen writes:

In Golwalkar's rendition, the secret of the Hindu community is that it cannot be defined, only felt. It is empty and inexpressible, a community of 'lack', but it is exactly this 'subtlety' that ennobles it. Throughout Golwalkar's writings the features of Hinduness, Hindu nation, and Hindu patriotism are all defined as in a state of 'becoming'.[15]

In the Savarkarite conception, hate and fear were instrumentalized against the other to form the national character. As the Gandhian national character dissipated by the 1960s, the Indian state became increasingly characterized by an anxious, insecure masculinity, even with a Congress government at the helm. Clearly, in the decades since independence, the Indian state has evolved in ways that are antithetical to Gandhi's *Surajya*.

In recent years, we have become preoccupied with either vigorously opposing or enthusiastically supporting the rehabilitation of Savarkar or Godse, whereas our real aim should be the rehabilitation, critically and empathetically, of Gandhian thought. The Gandhian doctrine was also about the practice of Sarvodaya—concern for the well-being for all—as a permanent antidote to hate and fear.

We return to Nair's Gandhi one last time: 'Who is Gandhi? Is he an implausible dream? Or a fable we might have heard?' To this, we add our own question: is Gandhi the moral compass that the nation needs today?

Which Gandhi did Godse and his compatriots kill? They killed a Gandhi who was not anti-state nor was he an anti-national. They killed a Gandhi who was an egalitarian. They killed a Gandhi who was a Hindu, a committed practitioner of ahimsa, and a deeply spiritual man.

In short, Godse and those whom he represented killed a Gandhi they completely misunderstood. Or perhaps they never had the ethical sensibility and the spiritual imagination that are necessary to understand him in the first place.

Acknowledgements

THIS book has been eight years in the making. It is not a tome, but all the same, collecting evidence from record rooms, bureaus and archives, and piecing them together, was a long, arduous, at times confusing process. However, it was a thrilling process of discovery, especially to see some facts in a new light. We have a lot of people to thank for guiding us through moments of doubt and supporting us in difficult times, of which the last two years have been the hardest.

This investigation would have never turned into a book if it was not for the encouragement of Seema Chishti. A friend and mentor, she was one of the first people to review our proposal and instil courage in us to move forward.

Understanding the extraordinary set of characters from Indian history would not have been possible without our teachers and scholars. Professor Dinesh Singh, former vice-chancellor, Delhi University, is, in our opinion, an underrated Gandhian scholar, whose understanding and appreciation of Mahatma Gandhi informed us in important ways. Among other things, Professor Singh made Gandhi and Gandhian thought accessible to us. We owe many thanks to Dr K.P. Shankaran, the former head of philosophy at St. Stephen's, for opening our eyes to the many versions of Gandhi. His conversations and writings forced us to revisit our one-dimensional understanding of Gandhi as the 'Father of the Nation'. In particular, he introduced us to Gandhi as an economic thinker. Oral history has been an important method of learning for us and Dr Rajeev Nair, professor of English at St. Stephen's, was a walking repository of literature, philosophy and politics.

The guiding light of our book is a friend, scholar and mentor who wishes to remain anonymous. Our conversations with them started at St. Stephen's and continue till date at the University of Cambridge. An authority on Hinduism, they suggested the most relevant readings and sourced them for us too. They also made critical comments, edits, and suggestions on the draft, which was invaluable to us. Their passion for understanding history and seeking knowledge is infectious. This work could not have been completed without them.

This book would also not have been possible without the help and resourcefulness of our unnamed sources, who helped us secure and navigate a vast number of documents. Thanks are also due to Rupak Kumar, who helped us access archival sources and sat through some of our deliberations. We would also like to thank Varghese George, a colleague and senior who kindly took the time to make critical comments on our first draft.

There are two unlikely people we owe a debt of gratitude to. Unfortunately, both have passed on. Arun Jaitley, former Union finance minister, and Dineshwar Sharma, former director, Intelligence Bureau. Mr Jaitley merits a special mention here, for he was always generous with his time and never shied away from discussing Gandhi, Savarkar and their conflicting ideologies. We disagreed a lot, but he respected dissenting voices and even welcomed differences of opinion, despite his ideological anchoring in Hindutva. He had, on occasion, remarked on the need to revisit history every now and then in order to understand the present.

We also owe thanks to Kapil Sibal, veteran Congress leader, for having many conversations about Gandhi and the relevance of his politics to us today.

Many thanks are due to our fellow journalists—Jayanth Jacob, Naresh Mathur, Sushant Singh and Liz Mathew—who have helped and supported us in various ways. Thanks are also due to the Chitrakoot Collective—Meera, Pavithra, Monika and Rachel—for their patience while we worked on the book. We would be remiss if we didn't mention Rajlaxmi Singh, a precocious preteen who told us how her generation views the Mahatma, a fakir-like figure whom they have only briefly encountered in books.

This book would have never seen the light of day if it wasn't for the drive of our editor, Swati Chopra. We thank her for her reserves of patience with us, and her formidable energy to make this happen. Thanks are also due to our copy editor, Amrita Mukerji.

We thank our families for their patience, especially over the last two years. We are lucky to be surrounded by our loved ones—Kabir, Ammu, Abhishek, Gayatri and Aditya, and the Vermas—who have taken on our share of responsibilities while we worked on the book. A special thanks to Ammu, for her luminous translation of V. Madhusoodanan Nair's poem on Gandhi.

Priyanka Kotamraju
Appu Esthose Suresh
New Delhi, August 2021

Endnotes

Prologue

1   'India After Independence', Chapter 10, *NCERT Social Sciences Textbook for Class 8*, (New Delhi: NCERT Publication Division) 2019.

2   S.K. Rudra, C.F. Andrews and M.K. Gandhi, *Economic & Political Weekly*, Vol. 37, Issue No. 34, 24 August 2002

3   K.P. Shankaran, via email to the authors, October 2016

4   https://www.youtube.com/watch?v=_Pc8WlNYp_0

5   Jeevan Lal Kapur Commission Report, Part 2, p. 321 and the Findings section of the same report. http://www.sacw.net/article2611.html

6   PTI, 'Mahatma Gandhi assassination records safe, says Rajnath Singh', Mint, 11 July 2014. https://www.livemint.com/Politics/5RPuVfOAzUWGljSHDlT3VI/Mahatma-Gandhi-assassination-records-safe-says-Rajnath-Sing.html

Book I: The Murderer

Chapter 1: The August Conspiracy

1   Air India's Traffic Department letter dated 2 April 1948 bearing file number: B0-17/2368/Jan B. The note mentions that on 8 August 1947, on the Bombay to Delhi service no. DN-438 (aircraft VT-AUG) three passengers travelled with the following names and ticket numbers: V. D. Savarkar (BDB.37509), N.D. Apte (BDB.34890) and N.V. Godse (BDB.37510). They carried four pieces of luggage weighing 75 lbs. On 9 April 1948, the Air India Traffic Department issued another letter bearing file number: B0-17/2654/JanB with the return flight details of the same three passengers on 11 August 1947.

2   Vikram Sampath, *Savarkar: Echoes from a Forgotten Past, 1883–1924* (New Delhi: Penguin Viking), 2019.

3   Ibid.

4   Manohar Malgonkar, *The Men Who Killed Gandhi* (Delhi: Lotus Roli, 1978), p. 43

5   Ibid., p. 46

6   A dossier in the form of a Confidential Note from the Poona Police dated 28 March 1948 bearing file number B/16/1148 detailing Godse's antecedence, known associations, history, family details, public profile and other details as part of intelligence gathering.

7   There are two views on this. It has been documented that Apte had a king's commission in the Royal Indian Air Force. (Malgonkar, *The Men Who Killed Gandhi*, p. 61-62.) However, former Defence Minister Manohar Parikkar informed the Supreme Court on 7 January 2016 that 'No information related Narayan Dattatray Apte being an airforce officer could be found anywhere.' (*The Hindu*, 15 November 2017. www.thehindu.com/news/national/mahatma-murder-supreme-court-told-aptes-identity-mired-in-doubt/article20450724.ece/amp/)

8   Manohar Malgonkar, *The Men Who Killed Gandhi* (Delhi: Lotus Roli, 1978), p. 66

9   Digambar Badge's statement in the Gandhi murder trial and his statement to the investigation team

10 Vinayak Damodar Savarkar's statement in the Gandhi murder trial.

11 Case Diary No 17-A submitted by Bal Kishan, Inspector of Police, CID, Delhi, from Gwalior, dated 16 February 1948

12 Ibid.

13 Statement by D.S. Parchure to City Inspector Madhav Singh, Lashkar, Gwalior on 17 February 1948

14 A.G. Noorani, 'Savarkar and Gandhi', *Frontline*, 28 March 2003

Chapter 2: The Accidental Breakthrough

1   Witness statements by Dr Sushila Nayyar as part of the Gandhi murder trial, Jeevan Lal Kapur Commission Report, Part I. http://www.sacw.net/article2611.html

2   Ibid.

3   Intelligence note dated 26 January 1948 shared with the director, Intelligence Bureau

4   Witness statements as part of the Gandhi murder trial

5   A top secret note of the Intelligence Bureau dated 20 July 1948 bearing File Number SA/716-II.

6   First Information Report no. 157 dated 6 June 1946, filed at the Faiz Bazar police station; Ramachandra Guha, *Gandhi: The Years that Changed the World*, 1914-1948, (New Delhi: Penguin Allen Lane), 2018, pp. 880-883

7   Walter Andersen, 'The Rashtriya Swayamsevak Sangh—II', *Economic & Political Weekly*, 18 March 1972

8   Deputy Superintendent Jaswant Singh, Case Diary 5 A, 3 February 1948

9   Deputy Superintendent Jaswant Singh, Case Diary no. 22, 1 February 1948

10 T.C.A. Raghavan, 'Origins and Development of Hindu Mahasabha Ideology—The Call of V.D. Savarkar and Bhai Parmanand', *Economic & Political Weekly*, 9 April 1983

Chapter 3: The Recruit

1   Aanchal Malhotra, *Remnants of a Separation: A History of Partition Through Material Memory*, Delhi: HarperCollins India, 2018
2   The Prabhakar examination was an exam conducted after matriculation, without the candidate having to go for a BA degree, particularly for the Punjab province
3   Madanlal Pahwa's statement to the court in the Gandhi murder trial
4   Ashis Nandy, 'Coming Home' in *Regimes of Narcissism, Regimes of Despair*, (New York: Oxford University Press), 2013
5   Madanlal Pahwa's statement to the court in the Gandhi murder trial
6   Ibid.
7   Ibid.
8   Aanchal Malhotra, *Remnants of a Separation: A History of Partition Through Material Memory*, Delhi: HarperCollins India, 2018
9   Madanlal Pahwa's statement to the court in the Gandhi murder trial
10 Ibid.
11 Ibid.
12 Madanlal Pahwa's statement to Bombay CID
13 Rita Kothari, *Unbordered Memories: Sindhi Stories of Partition*, (Delhi: Penguin Books India), 2009
14 Statement of Jagdish Chandra Jain to police and before the court in the Gandhi murder trial
15 Ibid.
16 Gyanendra Pandey, 'Partition and Independence in Delhi 1947-48', *Economic & Political Weekly*, 6 September 1997
17 Madanlal Pahwa's statement to the court in the Gandhi murder trial

Chapter 4: The Berretta Gun that Killed Gandhi

1   Witness statement of Madhukar Balkrishna Khire in the Gandhi murder trial

2 Witness statement of Madhukar Keshav Kale in the Gandhi murder trial

3 Case diary 16B from Bal Kishen, Inspector, Gwalior, 15-2-1948. Questioning of Madhukar Keshav Kale

4 M.A. Sreenivasan, *Of the Raj, the Maharajas, and Me*, (Sangam Books Ltd), 1991

5 D.S. Parchure's interrogation report. Statement by Parchure to the probe team on 16 February 1948

6 Ibid.

7 Witness statement of Mrs Angelina Coleston in the Gandhi murder trial

Book II: The Murderer

Chapter 1: An Open Secret

1 A Secret Note generated by the Tughlaq Road Police Station, Delhi, on 26 January 1948, Delhi Police, titled 'From the statement of Madan Lal, accused, it has been revealed that the following persons are directly or indirectly responsible for this offence:-'

2 Professor Jagdish Chandra Jain's witness statement in the Gandhi assassination case

3 Ibid.

4 Deputy Superintendent Jaswant Singh, Case Diary 5A, 3 February 1948.

5 Deputy Superintendent Jaswant Singh, Case Diary 22, 20 February 1948.

6 Intelligence Report generated by Delhi Police

7 Crime Report No. 25 dated 29 February 1948 by J.D. Nagarwala, Deputy Commissioner of Police, Special Branch, Bombay

8 Ibid.

9 J.D. Nagarwala, Deputy Commissioner of Police, Special Branch, Bombay, Case Diary, 1 February 1948

10 Ibid.

11 Ibid.

12 J.D. Nagarwala, Deputy Commissioner of Police, Special Branch, Bombay, Crime Report No 2, 31 January 1948

13 Ibid.

14 Professor Jagdish Chandra Jain's witness statement before the trial court

15 J.D. Nagarwala, Deputy Commissioner of Police, Special Branch, Bombay, Crime Report No. 7, 6 February 1948

16 J.D. Nagarwala Deputy Commissioner of Police, Special Branch, Bombay, Crime Report No. 25, 29 February 1948

17 Statement of V.D. Savarkar before Special Court Judge Atma Charan on 20 Novemeber 1948 in the Gandhi assassination case

18 Deputy Superintendent Jaswant Singh, Case Diary. 50, 20 March 1948

19 Statement of V.D. Savarkar before Special Court Judge Atma Charan on 20 Novemeber 1948 in the Gandhi assassination case

20 Ibid.

21 Statement of Narayan Apte before the Special Court Judge Atma Charan on 10 November 1948

22 Statement of V.D. Savarkar before Special Court Judge Atma Charan on 20 November 1948 in the Gandhi assassination case

23 Ibid.

Chapter 2: Alwar and the Princely Affair

1 Jeevan Lal Kapur Commission Report, Part 1. http://www.sacw.net/article2611.html

2 Jeevan Lal Kapur Commission Report. http://www.sacw.net/article2611.html

3 Secret note generated by DSP Jaswant Singh, 7 March 1948

4 Ibid.

5 Undated interrogation report by the Delhi Police

6 Ibid.

7   Jeevan Lal Kapur Commission Report. http://www.sacw.net/
    article2611.html
8   Ibid.
9   Delhi Police Interrogation Report, 3 February 1948
10 Ibid.
11 15 February Case Diary with statement of Nilkantha Dattatreya
    Parchure
12 15 February Case Diary with statement of Nilkantha Dattatreya
    Parchure
13 Report submitted by Inspector Bal Mukund on 6 February 1948
14 Jeevan Lal Kapur Commission Report. http://www.sacw.net/
    article2611.html
15 'Letter to Shriman Narayan on 1 December 1945' in *The Collected
    Works of Mahatma Gandhi*, Volume 88
16 'Letter to Sir Stafford Cripps on 12 April 1946' in *The Collected
    Works of Mahatma Gandhi*, Volume 90
17 *The Hindu*, 9 September 1945; 'Discussion with Narendra Dev and
    Suraj Prasad Awasthi' in *The Collected Works of Mahatma Gandhi*,
    Volume 88
18 Moonje Presidential Address, April 1944; Manu Bhagavan, 'Princely
    States and the Hindu Imaginary: Exploring the Cartography of
    Hindu Nationalism in Colonial India', Cambridge University Press,
    23 July 2008
19 *Harijan* article dated 4 August 1946 in *The Collected Works of
    Mahatma Gandhi*, Volume 91
20 Bhagavan, 23 July 2008
21 *Harijan* article dated 26 November 1946 in *The Collected Works of
    Mahatma Gandhi*, Volume 93
22 Manu Bhagavan, 'Princely States and the Hindu Imaginary:
    Exploring the Cartography of Hindu Nationalism in Colonial India',
    Cambridge University Press, 23 July 2008
23 Meeting between Gandhi and Lord Mountbatten on 4 April 1947 in
    The Collected Works of Mahatma Gandhi, Volume 94
24 Moonje Papers, Nehru Memorial Museum and Library

25   *The Collected Works of Mahatma Gandhi*, Volume 94
26   *The Collected Works of Mahatma Gandhi*, Volume 97
27   Ibid.
28   *The Collected Works of Mahatma Gandhi*, Volume 98

Chapter 3: The Militarization of the Hindus

1   Moonje Papers, Nehru Memorial Museum and Library
2   Ibid.
3   Ibid.
4   Ibid.
5   Ibid.
6   Ibid.
7   Ibid.
8   Ibid.
9   Ibid.
10   Moonje Papers and Hindu Mahasabha Papers, Nehru Memorial Museum and Library
11   Hindu Mahasabha Papers, Nehru Memorial Museum and Library
12   Ibid.
13   Ibid.
14   Ibid.

Book III: The Fakir

Chapter 1: Imagined Enemies

1   https://egazette.nic.in/WriteReadData/2019/214646.pdf
2   V.D. Savarkar, *Essentials of Hindutva* (Pune: Savarkar Bhavan), 1923. https://savarkar.org/en/encyc/2017/5/23/Essentials-of-Hindutva.html
3   Ibid.
4   Hindu Mahasabha papers, Nehru Memorial Museum and Library

5   Jawaharlal Nehru, *The Discovery of India* (new edition), (New Delhi: Penguin Books India), 2008

6   V.D. Savarkar, *Essentials of Hindutva* (Pune: Savarkar Bhavan), 1923. https://savarkar.org/en/encyc/2017/5/23/Essentials-of-Hindutva.html

7   Ankur Barua, 'Encountering Violence in Hindu Universes: Situating the Other on Vedic Horizons', *Journal of Religion and Violence*, Vol. 5, No. 1, 2017

8   Ibid.

9   Ibid.

10   Ibid.

11   Slavoj Žižek, 'Eastern Europe's Republics of Gilead', *New Left Review*, October 1990. https://newleftreview.org/issues/i183/articles/slavoj-zizek-eastern-europe-s-republics-of-gilead

Chapter 2: The Idea of Hindutva

1   Sushant Singh, 'The story of Faiz's Hum Dekhenge — from Pakistan to India, over 40 years', *Indian Express*, 27 December 2019. https://indianexpress.com/article/explained/the-story-of-faizs-hum-dekhenge-from-pakistan-to-india-over-40-years-caa-protest-6186565/; 'Hum Dekhenge' lyrics: https://www.rekhta.org/nazms/va-yabqaa-vajh-o-rabbik-hum-dekhenge-ham-dekhenge-faiz-ahmad-faiz-nazms; Markandey Katju, 'Why the Controversy Around Faiz's "Hum Dekhenge" Is So Fatuous', The Wire, 4 January 2020. https://thewire.in/communalism/faiz-hum-dekhenge-iit-kanpur

2   Yoginder Sikand, 'Iconoclasm: Not a Muslim Monopoly', Himal Mag, 13 February 2004. https://www.himalmag.com/iconoclasm-not-a-muslim-monopoly/; Richard M. Eaton, 'Temple Desecration and Muslim States in Medieval India', http://www.columbia.edu/itc/mealac/pritchett/00islamlinks/txt_eaton_temples2.pdf

3   Sumit Sarkar, *Modern India 1885-1947*, (Delhi: Laxmi Publications), 2008

4   Ibid.

5   K.N. Panikkar, *Against Lord and State: Religion and Peasant Uprisings in Malabar 1836-1921*, (Delhi: Oxford University Press), 1989

6   Thomas Blom Hansen, 'Recuperating Masculinity: Hindu nationalism, violence and the exorcism of the Muslim "Other"', Sage Journals, 1 June 1996. https://journals.sagepub.com/doi/10.1177/0308275X9601600203

7   Ibid.

Chapter 3: *Hindu Khatre Mein Hai*

1   U.N. Mukherji, *Is Hindu A Dying Race: A Social and Political Perspective of Hindu Reformers of Early 20th Century*, ed. Rakesh Sinha, (Kautilya), 2017

2   Ibid.

3   Foreword by Rakesh Sinha to U.N. Mukherji, *Is Hindu A Dying Race: A Social and Political Perspective of Hindu Reformers of Early 20th Century*, ed. Rakesh Sinha, (Kautilya), 2017

4   Jyoti Dwivedi, 'Fact Check: No, Muslims will not surpass Hindu population in India anytime soon', *India Today*, 22 October 2020. https://www.indiatoday.in/fact-check/story/fact-check-viral-post-muslim-population-india-1733926-2020-10-22

5   U.N. Mukherji, *Is Hindu A Dying Race: A Social and Political Perspective of Hindu Reformers of Early 20th Century*, ed. Rakesh Sinha, (Kautilya), 2017

6   Ibid.

7   Ibid.

8   Ibid.

9   Ankur Barua, 'Encountering Violence in Hindu Universes: Situating the Other on Vedic Horizons', *Journal of Religion and Violence*, Vol. 5, No. 1, 2017

10   Thomas Blom Hansen, 'Recuperating Masculinity: Hindu nationalism, violence and the exorcism of the Muslim "Other"', Sage Journals, 1 June 1996. https://journals.sagepub.com/doi/10.1177/0308275X9601600203

11   Hindu Mahasabha Papers, Nehru Memorial Museum and Library
12   *The Collected Works of Mahatma Gandhi, Volume 21,* 1920

Chapter 4: The Cult of Godse

1   PTI, 'BJP MP Pragya Thakur refers to Nathuram Godse as a 'patriot', yet again', *The Hindu,* 13 January 2021. https://tinyurl. com/93jh8kkh; Sudhi Ranjan Sen, 'BJP Lawmaker Sakshi Maharaj Calls Gandhi Assassin Nathuram Godse A "Patriot", Then Retracts', NDTV.com, 11 December 2014. https://tinyurl.com/28bnza7r; Sameer Yasir, 'Gandhi's killer evokes admiration as never before', *The New York Times,* 4 February 2020. https://tinyurl.com/5mzxfvd3; Ramachandra Guha, 'Godse worship goes mainstream in India', *Hindustan Times,* 1 June 2019. https://tinyurl.com/jk4cbwnf

2   Ramachandra Guha, 'Godse worship goes mainstream in India', *Hindustan Times,* 1 June 2019. https://tinyurl.com/jk4cbwnf

3   G.D. Khosla, *The Murder of the Mahatma And Other Cases from a Judge's Notebook,* (Mumbai: Jaico Books), 1963

4   G.D. Khosla, *The Murder of the Mahatma And Other Cases from a Judge's Notebook,* (Mumbai: Jaico Books), 1963

5   Nathuram Godse statement to the court in the Gandhi murder trial, read out also in the Panjab High Court

6   Nathuram Godse statement to the court of Justice Atma Charan in the Gandhi assassination case, the Red Fort Trial

7   Ibid.

8   Ibid.

9   Ibid.

10   Ibid.

11   Snigdhendu Bhattacharya, 'Congress divided Vande Mataram in 1937, and it led to Partition: Amit Shah', *Hindustan Times,* 27 June 2018. https://tinyurl.com/2rpujmar

12   Nathuram Godse statement to the court of Justice Atma Charan in the Gandhi assassination case, the Red Fort Trial

Epilogue

1   Nathuram Godse statement to the court of Justice Atma Charan in the Gandhi assassination case, the Red Fort Trial.

2   M.K. Gandhi, *Hind Swaraj or Indian Home Rule*, (Ahmedabad: Navjivan Publishing House). www.mkgandhi.org

3   Nathuram Godse statement to the court of Justice Atma Charan in the Gandhi assassination case, the Red Fort Trial.

4   Ibid.

5   Judith M. Brown and Anthony Parel (eds), *The Cambridge Companion to Gandhi*, (Cambridge: Cambridge University Press), 2011.

6   Moonje Papers, Nehru Memorial Museum and Library

7   'Discourse V and Verse 18', *The Bhagavad Gita According to Gandhi*, (US: North Atlantic Books), 2009.

8   K.P. Shankaran, 'Gandhi's Gita', *The Indian Express*, 30 January 2021. https://indianexpress.com/article/opinion/columns/mahatma-gandhi-gita-vaishnava-sect-hinduism-7166738/

9   M.K. Gandhi, *Constructive Programme, Its Meaning and Place*, originally published in 1941. www.mkgandhi.org

10 Ibid.

11 Ibid.

12 Ibid.

13 William L. Richter, 'Princes in Indian Politics', *Economic & Political Weekly*, Volume No. 6, Issue No. 9, 1971.

14 Subhash Mehta, 'Bhoodan-Gramdan Movement – 50 Years: A Review'. https://www.mkgandhi.org/vinoba/bhoodan.htm

15 Thomas Blom Hansen, *The Saffron Wave*, (Princeton: Princeton University Press), 1999

Index

Index

About the Authors

As an investigative journalist, **Appu Esthose Suresh** did extensive work on the changing pattern of communal riots in India, making a significant contribution towards understanding a sensitive and complex topic. Appu was recognized by the Mumbai Press Club's 2015 RedInk Awards in the 'Journalist of the Year' category for his series on the 'Communal Cauldron in Uttar Pradesh'. He has worked with the *Hindustan Times* as editor (special assignments), and at the *Indian Express* and *Mint*, among other publications. He was part of the International Consortium of Investigative Journalists team that investigated offshore accounts in British Virgin Islands and the HSBC Swiss accounts. He is currently Senior Atlantic Fellow at the International Inequalities Institute, London School of Economics & Political Science (LSE). He is also the founder of

Pixstory. He completed his studies from St. Stephen's College, New Delhi, and LSE.

Priyanka Kotamraju is a Gates Cambridge scholar pursuing a doctorate in sociology at the University of Cambridge, and a Senior Atlantic Fellow at the International Inequalities Institute at LSE. She was formerly editor of Khabar Lahariya, an award-winning grassroots media organization. She has also worked with the *Indian Express* and the *Hindu Business Line*. She is the co-founder of Chitrakoot Collective, a grassroots feminist research collective.